CW00350460

ST LUKE'S GOSPEL

ST LUKE'S
Gospel

A Commentary for Believers

THOMAS CREAN, O.P.
Foreword by Roy Schoeman

AROUCA PRESS

ISBN: 978-1-989905-92-0 (pbk)
ISBN: 978-1-989905-93-7 (hardcover)

Arouca Press
PO Box 55003
Bridgeport PO
Waterloo, ON N2J 3G0
Canada
www.aroucapress.com
Send inquiries to info@aroucapress.com

DEDICATION

*This book is dedicated to some sisters
who would doubtless prefer not to be named.*

CONTENTS

FOREWORD

IF "IGNORANCE OF THE SCRIPTURES IS IGNO-
rance of Christ, "as St. Jerome famously stated, it follows
that deepening one's understanding of scripture deepens
one's knowledge of, and intimacy with, Christ. Too often contemporary exegesis fails to help one do so, animated as it often
is by a spirit of criticism or a search for novelty. This is far from
the case with this book—as Fr. Crean states in his preface, he
"presupposes the dogmas of the faith". Since one of the dogmas
of the faith is that God is the author of Sacred Scripture[1], simple
respect for God as the author would require that one search for
meaning and significance in every word, both in the narrative
and in the words of Jesus, and this Fr. Crean has done, med-
itatively considering the text of St. Luke's Gospel line by line,
mining it for depths of meaning not apparent in a surface reading, or perhaps even after decades of such readings. Time after
time, small details in St. Luke's narrative that initially appear
irrelevant or even inconsistent are revealed to open up grand
vistas exposing mysteries about who Jesus is, the economy of
salvation, and the Jewish context in which salvation history
unfolded. At times these flow from careful attention to the
details included (or omitted) in the narrative, at times from
careful consideration of the statements, actions, or parables of
Jesus. Several times the author has provided a clear, compelling
interpretation of a parable which, until now, has remained an
enigma to me.

---

1   "These books are held by the Church as sacred and canonical . . . because,
written under the inspiration of the Holy Ghost, they have God for their
author, and have been transmitted to the Church as such" (First Vatican
Council, *The Dogmatic Constitution on the Catholic Faith*); "the Holy Ghost
Himself, by His supernatural power, stirred up and impelled the biblical writ-
ers to write, and assisted them while writing in such a manner that they conceived in their minds exactly, and determined to commit to writing faithfully,
and render in exact language, with infallible truth, all that God commanded
and nothing else; without that, God would not be the author of Scripture
in its entirety" (Pope Leo XIII, encyclical letter *Providentissimus Deus*).

The reader who enters into Fr. Crean's prayerful consideration of the inspired text of St. Luke's Gospel will be rewarded with a rich harvest of deepened understanding of Jesus' words and deeds, and hence, both a deeper understanding of the economy of salvation and a deeper relationship with Christ Himself.

Roy Schoeman,
author of *Salvation is from the Jews*
(Ignatius Press, 2004)

PREFACE

SINCE THERE ARE ALREADY SO MANY ANCIENT and modern commentaries on the gospels, I should not have thought of adding another, had not the superior of a religious community asked me to do so. I have called it a commentary 'for believers' because I presuppose the dogmas of the faith: unless he is engaged in apologetics, that is, seeking to prove these dogmas, I do not see how a Catholic exegete can rationally act otherwise.

I have tried to answer the questions that have occurred to me when reading St Luke's gospel. This has given rise to a commentary that is primarily literal, in St Thomas Aquinas's sense of the word, namely an explanation of the words spoken by the evangelist and by others. 'Literal' in this sense includes the allegorical meanings of parables. But since I have sometimes sought to discern, as far as I could, the *intentions* of our Lord, and since these intentions may include symbolising something by action, as well as expressing something by word, my commentary is to some extent also spiritual.

I have based my commentary on the Douay-Rheims version, as revised by the servant of God Richard Challoner. This is an accurate translation of the Vulgate; and the prevalence of the Vulgate from the patristic era onwards sufficiently shows, the Church being governed by the Spirit of truth, that it is a reliable expression of the written word of God. The Council of Trent, in declaring it authentic, was thus not simply establishing a fact but recognising one. While the Church could in the future declare some other translation of the Scriptures to be also authentic, she does not, it seems to me, have the power to 'de-authenticate' the Vulgate.

The brief opening section called 'about the author' contains ancient testimonies about the life of St Luke. I give them as I find them, without entering into a discussion of their authority. They are, at least, the Church's 'family traditions' about this saint, who, after St Paul wrote more of the New Testament than anyone else.

I am grateful to the Rev. John Hunwicke, of the Ordinariate of our Lady of Walsingham, for advice about some points of Greek usage, and to Fr Albert-Marie Crignon of the Fraternity of St Vincent Ferrer.

Thomas Crean, O. P.
Feast of our Lady of the Snows
AD 2021

ABOUT
THE AUTHOR

ST PAUL

"Luke, the most dear physician, saluteth you" (Col 4:14).

"There salute thee Epaphras, my fellow prisoner in Christ Jesus; Mark, Aristarchus, Demas, and Luke my fellow labourers" (Philem. 23–24).

"Demas hath left me, loving this world, and is gone to Thessalonica: Crescens into Galatia, Titus into Dalmatia. Only Luke is with me" (2 Tim. 4:9–11).

EUSEBIUS OF CAESAREA
(Church historian, born around AD 270)

"Luke, who was of Antiochian parentage and a physician by profession, and who was especially intimate with Paul and well acquainted with the rest of the apostles, has left us, in two inspired books, proofs of that spiritual healing art which he learned from them. One of these books is the Gospel, which he testifies that he wrote as those who were *from the beginning eyewitnesses and ministers of the word* delivered unto him, all of whom, as he says, he followed *diligently from the beginning*. The other book is the Acts of the Apostles which he composed not from the accounts of others, but from what he had seen himself" *(Ecclesiastical History*, Book 3.4).

ST EPIPHANIUS
(bishop of Salamis in Cyprus, born around 315)

"Luke was one of the seventy-two who had been scattered by the Saviour's saying.[2] But he was brought back to the Lord by St Paul and told to issue his gospel. He preached in Dalmatia, Gaul, Italy and Macedonia" *(Panarion*, 51.11).

---

2   This is a reference to Christ's telling the disciples in Capharnaum that they must eat His body and drink His blood.

ST GREGORY NAZIANZEN
(bishop and doctor of the Church, born around 330)
"Hadst thou no respect for the victims slain for Christ's sake? Didst thou not fear those mighty champions, that John, that Peter, Paul, James, Stephen, Luke, Andrew, and Thecla?" (*1st invective against Julian*, 69).

ST GAUDENTIUS
(bishop of Brescia in Italy from around 387)
"We possess relics of these four men (John the Baptist, Andrew, Thomas, and Luke). They preached the kingdom of God and justice, and though they were killed by unbelievers and wicked men, it is manifest by their miraculous operations that they are still living to God" (Sermon 17).

ST JEROME
(doctor of the Church, born around 342)
"Luke, a physician of Antioch, was not unskilled in the Greek language, as his writings indicate. An adherent of the apostle Paul, and companion of all his journeying, he wrote a Gospel, concerning which the same Paul says, *We send with him a brother whose praise in the gospel is among all the churches.* [...] He is buried at Constantinople to which city, in the twentieth year of Constantius, his bones together with the remains of Andrew the apostle were transferred" (*On Famous Men*, 7)

ST AUGUSTINE
(bishop and doctor of the Church, born 354)
"It appears to me, that of the various persons who have interpreted the living creatures in the Apocalypse to signify the four evangelists, those who have taken the lion to point to Matthew, the man to Mark, the calf to Luke, and the eagle to John, have made a more reasonable application of the figures than those who have assigned the man to Matthew, the eagle to Mark, and the lion to John. [...] But neither of the two parties has doubted but that Luke is signified by the calf, since this is the pre-eminent sacrifice made by a priest.

"For in that Gospel the narrator's account begins with Zacharias the priest. [...] It also records that the ceremonies belonging to the former priesthood were performed for the infant Christ; and if we carefully consider other things too, we find clearly that Luke directed his intention to the role of the priest (*Harmony of the Evangelists,* 1.6).

MENOLOGY OF EMPEROR BASIL II
(about AD 1000)

"Luke, born in Antioch, was a physician by profession and also a painter" (from the entry for October 18th).

DOMINICAN BREVIARY

"A great many people relate that he was a noted painter, and that he painted portraits of Christ and of the holy mother of God and of the apostles Peter and Paul. He lived to be eighty-four, remaining without a wife. Full of the Holy Ghost, he died in Bithynia" (from the entry for October 18th, 'taken from various early fathers').

ST THOMAS AQUINAS
(doctor of the Church, born around 1225)

"The apostles, led by an inward instinct of the Holy Ghost, handed down to the churches certain instructions that they did not put into writing, but which have been established in the Church by the constant practice of the faithful. Hence, the apostle says: *Stand fast, and hold the traditions which you have learned, whether by word*—that is, by word of mouth—*or by our epistle,* that is, by words put into writing. Among these traditions is the adoration of the image of Christ. Hence, it is said that Blessed Luke painted the image of Christ that is in Rome" (*Summa Theologiae*, 3a 25, 3 ad 4).

COMMENTARY
to the
GOSPEL OF ST. LUKE

1 Forasmuch as many have taken in hand to set forth in order a narration of the things that have been accomplished among us;

2 According as they have delivered them unto us, who from the beginning were eyewitnesses and ministers of the word:

3 It seemed good to me also, having diligently attained to all things from the beginning, to write to thee in order, most excellent Theophilus,

4 That thou mayest know the verity of those words in which thou hast been instructed.

5 There was in the days of Herod, the king of Judea, a certain priest named Zachary, of the course of Abia; and his wife was of the daughters of Aaron, and her name Elizabeth.

6 And they were both just before God, walking in all the commandments and justifications of the Lord without blame.

7 And they had no son, for that Elizabeth was barren, and they both were well advanced in years.

8 And it came to pass, when he executed the priestly function in the order of his course before God,

9 According to the custom of the priestly office, it was his lot to offer incense, going into the temple of the Lord.

10 And all the multitude of the people was praying without, at the hour of incense.

11 And there appeared to him an angel of the Lord, standing on the right side of the altar of incense.

12 And Zachary seeing him, was troubled, and fear fell upon him.

13 But the angel said to him: Fear not, Zachary, for thy prayer is heard; and thy wife Elizabeth shall bear thee a son, and thou shalt call his name John:

14 And thou shalt have joy and gladness, and many shall rejoice in his nativity.

15 For he shall be great before the Lord; and shall drink no wine nor strong drink: and he shall be filled with the Holy Ghost, even from his mother's womb.

VV. 1–25

THE THIRD GOSPEL BEGINS WITH THE CONception of St John the Baptist. St Luke could have gone back still further, and spoken of the conception and birth of the Blessed Virgin Mary. But he knew that these were things not yet to be spoken of publicly in the Church. "She hid herself in this world", says St Louis de Montfort, "having obtained of God and of His apostles and evangelists that she should not be made manifest".

St *Zachary* the priest and his wife St *Elizabeth* were Jews who kept the Old Law faithfully. St Thomas Aquinas tells us that the Old Law served three functions, for three different classes of people. For those who lived carelessly, it stopped them growing worse, in particular by keeping them from idolatry. For those who wanted to become good, it served for instruction. And for those who were already friends of God, the Law was a consolation. Zachary and Elizabeth belonged to this third and smallest group. St Robert Bellarmine remarks that the fact that they kept *all the commandments and justifications of the Lord without blame* refutes the error of those who suppose that the Law of Moses was impossible to observe.

There was only one temple in Israel, to signify that Christ would have only one Church. For this reason, each priest offered sacrifice only rarely. The rest of the time he taught or farmed, or had some other trade or profession. But now the *lot* fell to St Zachary to come to Jerusalem to burn *incense* in the Temple. This sacrifice of incense was offered twice a day, at morning and evening, on the golden altar in the Holy Place. In front of him, the priest could see the veil that covered the Holy of Holies, through which only the high priest could pass, and only once a year. Behind him was another veil, separating him from the people praying outside.

The angel appears at *the right side* of the golden altar. The right, in the Scriptures, signifies gladness. The long wait of the Jewish people for its Messias is coming to its end.

3

16 And he shall convert many of the children of Israel to the Lord their God.

17 And he shall go before him in the spirit and power of Elias; that he may turn the hearts of the fathers unto the children, and the incredulous to the wisdom of the just, to prepare unto the Lord a perfect people.

18 And Zachary said to the angel: Whereby shall I know this? for I am an old man, and my wife is advanced in years.

19 And the angel answering, said to him: I am Gabriel, who stand before God: and am sent to speak to thee, and to bring thee these good tidings.

20 And behold, thou shalt be dumb, and shalt not be able to speak until the day wherein these things shall come to pass, because thou hast not believed my words, which shall be fulfilled in their time.

21 And the people were waiting for Zachary; and they wondered that he tarried so long in the temple.

22 And when he came out, he could not speak to them: and they understood that he had seen a vision in the temple. And he made signs to them, and remained dumb.

23 And it came to pass, after the days of his office were accomplished, he departed to his own house.

24 And after those days, Elizabeth his wife conceived, and hid herself five months, saying:

25 Thus hath the Lord dealt with me in the days wherein he hath had regard to take away my reproach among men.

26 And in the sixth month, the angel Gabriel was sent from God into a city of Galilee, called Nazareth,

27 To a virgin espoused to a man whose name was Joseph, of the house of David; and the virgin's name was Mary.

28 And the angel being come in, said unto her: Hail, full of grace, the Lord is with thee: blessed art thou among women.

29 Who having heard, was troubled at his saying, and thought with herself what

Why does St Gabriel say that the Baptist will come *in the spirit and power of Elias*? Elias admonished a king; St John the Baptist will do the same. Elias fasted for forty days; John will be a great ascetic from childhood. Elias showed the people on Mount Carmel that the Lord and not Baal is God; John will point out Jesus Christ.

St John the Baptist will *turn the hearts of the fathers unto the children*. By his preaching, some of the Jews will be made ready for the Messias, and so the prayers of those who have gone before, that God would send the world a Saviour, can be heard: the prayers of the fathers will now benefit the children. And the souls of these fathers themselves, waiting in Limbo, will learn about the effect of the Baptist's preaching and their charity toward their descendants will be the more stirred up.

His preaching will yield an effect even beyond Israel: the pagans, those who are now *incredulous*, without faith in the word of God, will learn about the prophecies, which are *the wisdom of the just*, and see that they have been fulfilled.

Why must St Zachary suffer dumbness after his doubt? Having hesitated to accept the words of God, it is fitting that he lose for a time the use of human words. But St John, who will call himself a voice, will return a voice to his father. Zachary will be grateful to him, God in this way granting that Zachary himself will fulfil the very prophecy which he doubted, his father's heart being turned toward his son.

St Elizabeth *hides herself* when she conceives. In her humility, she does not want people to congratulate her on the greatness of the favour she has received from God.

vv. 26–38

The Blessed Virgin was already *espoused*, that is, married to St Joseph. If she is sometimes spoken of as simply 'betrothed' to him, this is to show the purity of their marriage. It is reasonable also to suppose that she was already living in the house of St Joseph, so that no imputations would be cast upon her once she had conceived her Child.

manner of salutation this should be.

30 And the angel said to her: Fear not, Mary, for thou hast found grace with God.

31 Behold thou shalt conceive in thy womb, and shalt bring forth a son; and thou shalt call his name Jesus.

32 He shall be great, and shall be called the Son of the most High; and the Lord God shall give unto him the throne of David his father; and he shall reign in the house of Jacob for ever.

33 And of his kingdom there shall be no end.

34 And Mary said to the angel: How shall this be done, because I know not man?

35 And the angel answering, said to her: The Holy Ghost shall come upon thee, and the power of the most High shall overshadow thee. And therefore also the Holy which shall be born of thee shall be called the Son of God.

36 And behold thy cousin Elizabeth, she also hath conceived a son in her old age; and this is the sixth month with her that is called barren:

37 Because no word shall be impossible with God.

38 And Mary said: Behold the handmaid of the Lord; be it done to me according to thy word. And the angel departed from her.

St Gabriel does not need to say to her, *Fear not,* as soon as he appears, as he had done to Zachary. Living in perfect union with the Creator, Mary is not frightened by the sight of one of His servants. He says, *Fear not,* only once he has greeted her with high praise. Since she lives habitually in the thought of her own nothingness before God, this praise was able to trouble her.

In speaking to St Joseph, the angel says that Jesus will *save his people from their sins.* Why does he not say this to our Lady? Perhaps because she had no sins, and thus he would have been saying something that was less pertinent to her. Instead, he tells her three times that her Son will be a king: He will have *the throne of David, reign in the house of Jacob,* and have dominion with *no end.* Implicit in this is the promise of her own queenship: in the Old Testament, which foreshadowed the New, it was always the mother of the king who was the queen.

Our Lady knew from the Scriptures that the Messias was to be born of a Virgin. Why then does she remind the angel of her vow of virginity, saying *I know not man,* as if this were a difficulty? Perhaps because the prophecy of Isaias had not said how the virgin would conceive and bear; perhaps too, so that the angel might ratify the word of the prophet. The Law taught that two witnesses were sufficient to establish any truth.

The Holy which shall be born of thee: we could also translate the angel's words: "The one who shall be born of thee in a holy way", and miraculously. In this way, the answer would correspond more closely to the question, as an assurance that not even in giving birth would she lose her virginity.

Mary did not doubt St Gabriel's words, as Zachary had done. Therefore, he rewards her faith with a secondary proof: God's power as manifested in Elizabeth's conception. She does not need this proof, since her faith rests on the word of God alone: but it is a gracious gift to her.

In the Old Testament, the angel of the Lord departs from Gedeon and Manue with fire; from Mary he departs quietly, as befits a servant.

39 And Mary rising up in those days, went into the hill country with haste into a city of Judea.

40 And she entered into the house of Zachary, and saluted Elizabeth.

41 And it came to pass, that when Elizabeth heard the salutation of Mary, the infant leaped in her womb. And Elizabeth was filled with the Holy Ghost:

42 And she cried out with a loud voice, and said: Blessed art thou among women, and blessed is the fruit of thy womb.

43 And whence is this to me, that the mother of my Lord should come to me?

44 For behold as soon as the voice of thy salutation sounded in my ears, the infant in my womb leaped for joy.

45 And blessed art thou that hast believed, because those things shall be accomplished that were spoken to thee by the Lord.

46 And Mary said: My soul doth magnify the Lord.

47 And my spirit hath rejoiced in God my Saviour.

48 Because he hath regarded the humility of his handmaid; for behold from henceforth all generations shall call me blessed.

49 Because he that is mighty, hath done great things to me; and holy is his name.

50 And his mercy is from generation unto generations, to them that fear him.

51 He hath shewed might in his arm: he hath scattered the proud in the conceit of their heart.

52 He hath put down the mighty from their seat, and hath exalted the humble.

53 He hath filled the hungry with good things; and the rich he hath sent empty away.

54 He hath received Israel his servant, being mindful of his mercy:

55 As he spoke to our fathers, to Abraham and to his seed for ever.

56 And Mary abode with her about three months; and she returned to her own house.

vv. 39–56

Christ begins His work of sanctification through His mother. At her *greeting*, He fills John *with the Holy Ghost* as the angel had foretold. By a miracle, John receives the power to recognise the Saviour and so to *leap for joy*. St Elizabeth receives the power to recognise Mary as *the mother of my Lord*; the mother of that same Lord whose words she knows that Mary has believed.

Before recording Mary's prophecy, the Magnificat, St Luke does not say that she was filled with the Holy Spirit or instructed by Him, as he does when recording the prophecies of Elizabeth, Zachary, and Simeon. No doubt this is because she was always so filled.

The Blessed Virgin calls God her *Saviour*. At the first moment of her existence, the Holy Spirit overshadowed her, so that she did not inherit the sin of Adam. Thus, she is conscious of having been saved.

She speaks literally of her 'lowliness'; yet humility is also a good translation, since her to be aware of one's lowliness *is* humility. This humility drew the eternal Word to Mary.

Having spoken of what God has done for her, her thoughts turn to what He has previously done in heaven. *He hath scattered the proud* angels, especially Lucifer, who imagined that he could make himself like to God. *He hath put down the mighty* angels who rebelled against Him, and *exalted the humble* ones who submitted to His law.[1] Her words also suggest that the possession of temporal power makes it more difficult for men also to obtain salvation. But there is no reason to see them as meaning that such power itself is now to change hands, since this is not a part of the promises of the gospel. As one of the Church's hymns for Epiphany says: "He does not snatch away mortal crowns, who gives heavenly ones".

Under the Old Testament, God promised temporal prosperity to the Jews who kept the Law. This promise is not given to Christians, since wealth is liable to obstruct the higher perfection to

---

1 Both Cardinal Cajetan and Venerable Mary of Agreda thus interpret these words.

57 Now Elizabeth's full time of being delivered was come, and she brought forth a son.

58 And her neighbours and kinsfolks heard that the Lord had shewed his great mercy towards her, and they congratulated her.

59 And it came to pass, that on the eighth day they came to circumcise the child, and they called him by his father's name, Zachary.

60 And his mother answering, said: Not so; but he shall be called John.

61 And they said to her: There is none of thy kindred that is called by this name.

62 And they made signs to his father, how he would have him called.

63 And demanding a writing table, he wrote, saying: John is his name. And they all wondered.

64 And immediately his mouth was opened, and his tongue loosed, and he spoke, blessing God.

65 And fear came upon all their neighbours; and all these things were noised abroad over all the hill country of Judea.

66 And all they that had heard them laid them up in their heart, saying: What an one, think ye, shall this child be? For the hand of the Lord was with him.

67 And Zachary his father was filled with the Holy Ghost; and he prophesied, saying:

68 Blessed be the Lord God of Israel; because he hath visited and wrought the redemption of his people:

69 And hath raised up an horn of salvation to us, in the house of David his servant:

70 As he spoke by the mouth of his holy prophets, who are from the beginning:

which the gospel calls the faithful. Our Lady seems to prophesy this change here in what she says of *the rich*.

She compares Israel to a child whom his father lifts into his arms, acknowledging the child as his own. This refers principally to *the Israel of God* of whom St Paul will speak: all who believe in the Messias who has now arrived.

We need not suppose that our Lady travelled alone; it is quite possible that St Joseph accompanied her there and back, even if he did not remain during the *three months* in Zachary's house.

vv. 57–80

St John is the bridge between the old and the new. He is born to a priest of the old Law, but receives a name that refers to the new. 'John' means 'the grace of the Lord'.

Zachary is inspired to recognise the Blessed Virgin as the mother of the Redeemer. Jesus is the *horn of salvation,* that is, 'the mighty Saviour', who belongs to the *house of David*, both legally by reason of St Joseph and physically by virtue of Mary. Zachary's words cannot refer to his own son: John the Baptist does not belong to the house of David, since Zachary and Elizabeth are descendants of Levi, not of Judah the ancestor of David.

The birth of the Saviour was prophesied by the *holy prophets who are from the beginning*. Even before the Flood there were prophets, though very few of their words have been preserved. He saves us in particular from the evil spirits, who are most of all *our enemies* who *hate us*. By baptism we are *delivered from* their *hand*.

St Zachary, filled with the Holy Ghost, receives knowledge of the divinity of Jesus Christ. He prophesies that the Baptist will go before the *face of the Lord*, until they meet on the banks of the Jordan. He also calls Christ *the Orient*, that is, the rising one. Like the rising of the sun, our Lord's conception and birth take place by no human power, foreshadowing His future Resurrection. This divine Sun will enlighten both the just who *sit in darkness* in Limbo, and the ignorant upon earth.

11

71 Salvation from our enemies, and from the hand of all that hate us:

72 To perform mercy to our fathers, and to remember his holy testament,

73 The oath, which he swore to Abraham our father, that he would grant to us,

74 That being delivered from the hand of our enemies, we may serve him without fear,

75 In holiness and justice before him, all our days.

76 And thou, child, shalt be called the prophet of the most High: for thou shalt go before the face of the Lord to prepare his ways:

77 To give knowledge of salvation to his people, unto the remission of their sins:

78 Through the bowels of the mercy of our God, in which the Orient from on high hath visited us:

79 To enlighten them that sit in darkness, and in the shadow of death: to direct our feet into the way of peace.

80 And the child grew, and was strengthened in spirit; and was in the deserts until the day of his manifestation to Israel.

We do not know at what age John went into the desert, but St Luke's words suggest that it was when he was still a *child*, and thus that he was sustained there by divine and angelic aid.

1 And it came to pass, that in those days there went out a decree from Caesar Augustus, that the whole world should be enrolled.

2 This enrolling was first made by Cyrinus, the governor of Syria.

3 And all went to be enrolled, every one into his own city.

4 And Joseph also went up from Galilee, out of the city of Nazareth into Judea, to the city of David, which is called Bethlehem: because he was of the house and family of David,

5 To be enrolled with Mary his espoused wife, who was with child.

6 And it came to pass, that when they were there, her days were accomplished, that she should be delivered.

7 And she brought forth her firstborn son, and wrapped him up in swaddling clothes, and laid him in a manger; because there was no room for them in the inn.

8 And there were in the same country shepherds watching, and keeping the night watches over their flock.

9 And behold an angel of the Lord stood by them, and the brightness of God shone round about them; and they feared with a great fear.

10 And the angel said to them: Fear not; for, behold, I bring you good tidings of great joy, that shall be to all the people:

11 For, this day, is born to you a Saviour, who is Christ the Lord, in the city of David.

12 And this shall be a sign unto you. You shall find the infant wrapped in swaddling clothes, and laid in a manger.

13 And suddenly there was with the angel a multitude of the heavenly army, praising God, and saying:

14 Glory to God in the highest; and on earth peace to men of good will.

15 And it came to pass, after the angels departed from them into heaven, the shepherds said one to another: Let us go over to Bethlehem, and let us see this word that is come to pass, which the Lord hath shewed to us.

16 And they came with haste; and they found Mary and

VV. 1–20

ITH *THE DECREE FROM CAESAR AUGUSTUS* begins the mysterious relation between the Church and the temporal power of Rome. This relation was foreshadowed in the Old Testament, when the people of the Romans made covenant with Judas Machabeus. Now, the first emperor of the Romans sets in motion by an official act the events leading to the birth of the Saviour of the world. To reward this act, not only will divine providence watch over the empire, but more than this, God will make the emperors in due time the chief temporal protectors of the Church. Hence many of the Fathers have foretold that antichrist could not come for as long as a Roman imperial power remained on earth.[1]

Joseph and Mary go together to *Bethlehem*, which means 'the House of Bread'. There, our Lady *brought forth* her Son. St Gregory Nazianzen calls this birth a miracle beyond man's comprehension. It fulfilled the prophecy of Isaias: *Before she was in labour, she brought forth*. He is called *her first-born Son,* because there was none before, not because there was to be another afterward; also, because there were special legal obligations attaching to the first-born son; and finally, because He is *the first-born of every creature,* as it were the elder brother of all created things.

By noting that Mary herself *wrapped him up in swaddling clothes*, St Luke delicately suggests the miraculous and painless character of the birth.

The angel who evangelises the shepherds first strikes them with *great fear*. Thus taken out of themselves, they are ready to learn the mystery of the incarnation: the Saviour and Messias who has been born is also the LORD whom Israel has long

---

1   The Roman empire ended in the East in 1453, a life-time before the outbreak of the Reformation. In the West, the title of holy Roman emperor was renounced in 1806, but the imperial house continued to reign until Blessed Charles of Austria was driven out by his enemies in 1918. His eldest son, the last heir apparent, died in 2011.

Joseph, and the infant lying in the manger.

17 And seeing, they understood of the word that had been spoken to them concerning this child.

18 And all that heard, wondered; and at those things that were told them by the shepherds.

19 But Mary kept all these words, pondering them in her heart.

20 And the shepherds returned, glorifying and praising God, for all the things they had heard and seen, as it was told unto them.

21 And after eight days were accomplished, that the child should be circumcised, his name was called JESUS, which was called by the angel, before he was conceived in the womb.

22 And after the days of her purification, according to the law of Moses, were accomplished, they carried him to Jerusalem, to present him to the Lord:

23 As it is written in the law of the Lord: Every male opening the womb shall be called holy to the Lord:

24 And to offer a sacrifice, according as it is written in the law of the Lord, a pair of turtledoves, or two young pigeons:

worshipped. This *great joy shall be for all the people*, that is, for the new people who are now coming to be. Shepherds are chosen to represent this people, as the Holy Spirit will appoint shepherds to represent His people in every age.

Why is *the infant wrapped in swaddling clothes and lying in a manger* a 'sign'? Perhaps the contrast between the fine swaddling clothes which Mary has woven with her own hands and the poverty of the manger is a sign of how extremes meet, by the Incarnation. Also, He lies in a manger to show that He will be the food of believers; of all the faithful beasts of burden, says St Augustine.

The angel foretells that *peace* will come *to men of good will*. Is this a reference to a good will in them or in God? To both: peace comes to those who have been made good by God's good will.

V. 21

Jewish boys had to be circumcised *after eight days*. This was to symbolise the resurrection of Christ, on the day after the sabbath, when He was freed from mortality.

St Bernard notes that it was at the circumcision that Jesus first shed His precious blood. Therefore it is fitting that He is first called by His *name* on this day, since His name means 'Saviour', and we are saved by that blood.

VV. 22–24

Our Lady was not subject to the law of *purification,* since according to Leviticus only women who had conceived by a man were so subject. Yet she wishes to accomplish this law nevertheless, to show her love for God who instituted it, and from humility; and also, says one of the earliest fathers, so that the mystery of her virginity would be hidden from the prince of this world.

In accord with the law of purification, Mary and Joseph offer the sacrifice of the poor, *a pair of turtledoves*. Those who could afford it would have offered a lamb. But could they not have used the gold which the magi had brought them? Presumably they had already given it away: the Church calls St Joseph

25 And behold there was a man in Jerusalem named Simeon, and this man was just and devout, waiting for the consolation of Israel; and the Holy Ghost was in him.

26 And he had received an answer from the Holy Ghost, that he should not see death, before he had seen the Christ of the Lord.

27 And he came by the Spirit into the temple. And when his parents brought in the child Jesus, to do for him according to the custom of the law,

28 He also took him into his arms, and blessed God, and said:

29 Now thou dost dismiss thy servant, O Lord, according to thy word in peace;

30 Because my eyes have seen thy salvation,

31 Which thou hast prepared before the face of all peoples:

32 A light to the revelation of the Gentiles, and the glory of thy people Israel.

33 And his father and mother were wondering at those things which were spoken concerning him.

34 And Simeon blessed them, and said to Mary his mother: Behold this child is set for the fall, and for the resurrection of many in Israel, and for a sign which shall be contradicted;

35 And thy own soul a sword shall pierce, that, out of many hearts, thoughts may be revealed.

36 And there was one Anna, a prophetess, the daughter of Phanuel, of the tribe of Asher; she was far advanced in years, and had lived with her husband seven years from her virginity.

37 And she was a widow until fourscore and four years; who departed not from the temple, by fastings and prayers serving night and day.

38 Now she, at the same hour, coming in, confessed to the Lord; and spoke of him to all that looked for the redemption of Israel.

Amator paupertatis, 'lover of poverty'. Also, it would have been incongruous for them to have led an irrational lamb to the temple when they carried the Lamb of God in their arms.

Every male opening the womb is a Hebrew way of saying 'every male child who is the first-born'.

vv. 25–40

Why does *Israel* need *consolation*? Because its territory is occupied by Roman armies? Much more, because faith is weak where it should most excel: the chief priests and scribes, though they tell the magi to seek the Messias in Bethlehem, do not trouble to seek Him out themselves. But Simeon is faithful, and *the consolation of Israel* may be his title for the Messias.

It is said that the body of St Simeon is incorrupt, in a church in Croatia. If it remains so until the end, then this will be a second fulfilment of the promise that *he should not see death before he had seen the Christ.*

The evangelist says that Mary and Joseph offered the birds for the law of purification, but not that they paid the money for the law of ransoming the first-born. Perhaps this is because it would be incongruous if the Redeemer were shown to be redeemed.

The Child is not only *a light to the revelation of the gentiles* but also *the glory of Israel*; like Simeon, Israel may at last be at peace, knowing that it has accomplished that for which God chose it.

Having spoken of the salvation which Jesus would offer mankind, St Simeon now speaks to our Lady about the response which men would make. This is why this meeting is both one of the joyful mysteries of the rosary and one of Mary's seven sorrows. For although *many in Israel* will believe and *rise* from their sins, many also will *fall* further from God: for these latter, Christ will be *a sign which shall be contradicted*, especially when He takes to Himself the Cross whose power they deny. During His life-time and afterwards, many in Israel will shun this sign of the Cross.

The *sword* which *shall pierce* Mary's *soul* is that of which St Paul speaks, as *reaching unto the division of the soul and the spirit*. The 'soul' signifies our natural love and understanding; the 'spirit'

39 And after they had performed all things according to the law of the Lord, they returned into Galilee, to their city Nazareth.

40 And the child grew, and waxed strong, full of wisdom; and the grace of God was in him.

41 And his parents went every year to Jerusalem, at the solemn day of the pasch,

42 And when he was twelve years old, they going up into Jerusalem, according to the custom of the feast,

43 And having fulfilled the days, when they returned, the child Jesus remained in Jerusalem; and his parents knew it not.

44 And thinking that he was in the company, they came a day's journey, and sought him among their kinsfolks and acquaintance.

45 And not finding him, they returned into Jerusalem, seeking him.

46 And it came to pass, that, after three days, they found him in the temple, sitting in the midst of the doctors, hearing them, and asking them questions.

47 And all that heard him were astonished at his wisdom and his answers.

signifies the love and understanding breathed into us by the Holy Ghost. Our Lady, standing near the Cross, will sacrifice her natural love for her Son in order to offer Him to the Father for the salvation of mankind. This is her work of co-redemption.

St Simeon's words about the sword do not form a parenthesis in his prophecy. Together with his words about Christ as the sign of contradiction they lead to its conclusion. *The thoughts out of many hearts*, that is, out of the hearts of all mankind, will *be revealed* on the day of Judgement, when men are shown to have accepted or refused redemption: that redemption which the Son and the mother will both have offered, He as the one Redeemer and she as co-redemptrix.

Anna belongs to *the tribe of Asher*. Before Moses died, he addressed this tribe, saying: *As the days of thy youth, so also shall thy old age be.* In this respect, Asher represents Israel: just as Israel was in covenant with God when she was young, so it is believed that she will receive the gospel in her old age, that is, toward the end of the world. Anna symbolises this by her own life: she had a husband for seven years when she was young, then spent many years alone, and now, in her old age, she meets the Man of the new covenant.

vv. 41–52

St Joseph was obliged, like other adult males, to attend the three great feasts at Jerusalem: the *Pasch* (Passover), Pentecost and Tabernacles. The women were not obliged to attend. Hence, it is as an act of devotion that the Blessed Virgin accompanies her spouse for the Pasch.

Given the love which they had for Jesus, it may well have been by divine power that He came to be separated from them at the end of the feast. One author states that they received graces of contemplation which partially separated them from their senses, so that they did not notice His departure.

Why does He not tell them before leaving? Partly as a sign that His subjection to them is not like that of other children to their parents. As a divine Person, Christ had the right to withdraw this subjection at any time. Partly, also, He does it

48 And seeing him, they wondered. And his mother said to him: Son, why hast thou done so to us? behold thy father and I have sought thee sorrowing.

49 And he said to them: How is it that you sought me? did you not know, that I must be about my father's business?

50 And they understood not the word that he spoke unto them.

51 And he went down with them, and came to Nazareth, and was subject to them. And his mother kept all these words in her heart.

52 And Jesus advanced in wisdom, and age, and grace with God and men.

---

again that they did not immediately understand. They had feared, no doubt, that Herod's son Archelaus had seized Him, and that the time of His passion had come upon Him already.

Perhaps, also, they are said not to understand because the symbolic nature of His action was hidden from them. For "that which is His Father's" means also the Father's plan of salvation, according to which His Son would die and rise again and ascend into heaven. It is as if Christ is saying: "Why be surprised if I am doing now in a symbol that which I will do in all truth when the time comes?" The Christ must suffer and die, and be removed from human sight, and so enter into His Father's house.

so that they may be more abandoned to divine providence, like Abraham when he was told to sacrifice Isaac, only to receive him back on the third day (Gen. 22:4). In particular, the Lord is preparing Mary for a later occasion, when again they will be separated in Jerusalem, and again she will find Him *after three days*.

What *questions* did the boy Jesus put to *the doctors of the law*, and what were His *answers*? Some authors think that the subject of discussion on that day was the Messias: when he would come and what he would do.[2] Isaias says: *As the rain and the snow come down from heaven, and return no more thither, but soak the earth, and water it, and make it to spring, and give seed to the sower, and bread to the eater, so shall my word be, which shall go forth from my mouth.* With the modesty suitable for a boy among the doctors of the law in the sacred precincts of the temple, He who is the Word of the Father begins to water their hearts with His teaching, planting the seeds that may grow later into an explicit faith in Him as the Messias of Israel.

If his parents *wondered* at what they saw, this was not because they were surprised by His wisdom, since they knew that He is the true Son of God, but because He had never publicly displayed it before in such a way.

Our Lady, speaking of herself and St Joseph, refers to herself only after her spouse: *thy Father and I*. She seems in her humility to have invented this custom.[3]

Why do Mary and Joseph not understand Christ's reply, *I must be about my Father's business*, or, more literally, "in that which is my Father's"? They knew, after all, that He had come from heaven to bring His Father's message of salvation to the world. Perhaps it was simply because they were so full of joy to see Him

2 A modern French convert from Judaism has recorded his experience of rabbinical school in Israel, and of how the rabbis have a rather informal style of teaching in comparison to what happens in a French university, allowing their disciples to interrupt them and to express their own opinions. Jean-Marie Elie Setbon, *From the Kippah to the Cross* (Ignatius Press, 2015).
3 Ronald Knox, a fine scholar of Greek and Latin literature and a translator of the bible, remarks that nowhere in the Old Testament or in pagan antiquity is it found, when a person speaks of himself and another together, that he mentions the other person first.

1 Now in the fifteenth year of the reign of Tiberius Caesar, Pontius Pilate being governor of Judea, and Herod being tetrarch of Galilee, and Philip his brother tetrarch of Iturea, and the country of Trachonitis, and Lysanias tetrarch of Abilina;

2 Under the high priests Annas and Caiphas; the word of the Lord was made unto John, the son of Zachary, in the desert.

3 And he came into all the country about the Jordan, preaching the baptism of penance for the remission of sins;

4 As it was written in the book of the sayings of Isaias the prophet: A voice of one crying in the wilderness: Prepare ye the way of the Lord, make straight his paths.

5 Every valley shall be filled; and every mountain and hill shall be brought low; and the crooked shall be made straight; and the rough ways plain;

6 And all flesh shall see the salvation of God.

7 He said therefore to the multitudes that went forth to be baptized by him: Ye offspring of vipers, who hath shewed you to flee from the wrath to come?

8 Bring forth therefore fruits worthy of penance; and do not begin to say, We have Abraham for our father. For I say unto you, that God is able of these stones to raise up children to Abraham.

9 For now the axe is laid to the root of the trees. Every tree therefore that bringeth not forth good fruit, shall be cut down and cast into the fire.

10 And the people asked him, saying: What then shall we do?

11 And he answering, said to them: He that hath two coats, let him give to him that hath none; and he that hath meat, let him do in like manner.

12 And the publicans also came to be baptized, and said to him: Master, what shall we do?

13 But he said to them: Do nothing more than that which is appointed you.

14 And the soldiers also asked him, saying: And what shall we do? And he said to them:

VV. 1–20

WE MAY BE SURPRISED THAT ST JOHN THE Baptist speaks so severely to those who come to him for baptism. Evidently, he perceives that they were not sincere. From St Matthew's gospel, we learn that it was above all the Pharisees and Sadducees to whom he gave this warning. Perhaps going to see the strangely dressed prophet by the Jordan had become the fashionable thing to do; or perhaps they wished to receive this baptism as an easy way to bolster their reputation for religion among the people.

A time of judgement has come for Israel. Those who do not believe in the Messias will find themselves *cut down*, that is, cut off from God's people. St John tells the crowds, the tax-gatherers and the soldiers that they can prepare themselves to receive the grace of faith by performing corporal works of mercy and doing the duties of their particular state in life.

There was a general expectation that the Messias was near, since a prophecy of Daniel indicated that the time had come.

The baptism of St John did not communicate divine grace, but prepared people to receive the baptism of Christ. In that respect it was like one of the sacramentals of the new Law, by making good use of which we are better disposed to receive the sacraments. By contrast, the baptism of Christ, by its own power infuses into the hearts of those who receive it the *Holy Ghost*, who always comes with the *fire* of divine love.

What is the winnowing *fan* which St John sees in the *hand* of our Lord? It seems to be the authority to judge which the Son has received from the Father.

Do violence to no man; neither calumniate any man; and be content with your pay.

15 And as the people were of opinion, and all were thinking in their hearts of John, that perhaps he might be the Christ;

16 John answered, saying unto all: I indeed baptize you with water; but there shall come one mightier that I, the latchet of whose shoes I am not worthy to loose: he shall baptize you with the Holy Ghost, and with fire:

17 Whose fan is in his hand, and he will purge his floor, and will gather the wheat into his barn; but the chaff he will burn with unquenchable fire.

18 And many other things exhorting, did he preach to the people.

19 But Herod the tetrarch, when he was reproved by him for Herodias, his brother's wife, and for all the evils which Herod had done;

20 He added this also above all, and shut up John in prison.

21 Now it came to pass, when all the people were baptized, that Jesus also being baptized and praying, heaven was opened;

22 And the Holy Ghost descended in a bodily shape, as a dove upon him; and a voice came from heaven: Thou art my beloved Son; in thee I am well pleased.

23 And Jesus himself was beginning about the age of thirty years; being (as it was supposed) the son of Joseph, who was of Heli, who was of Mathat,

24 Who was of Levi, who was of Melchi, who was of Janne, who was of Joseph,

25 Who was of Mathathias, who was of Amos, who was of Nahum, who was of Hesli, who was of Nagge,

26 Who was of Mahath, who was of Mathathias, who was of Semei, who was of Joseph, who was of Juda,

27 Who was of Joanna, who was of Reza, who was of Zorobabel, who was of Salathiel, who was of Neri,

28 Who was of Melchi, who was of Addi, who was of Cosan, who was of Helmadan, who was of Her,

29 Who was of Jesus, who was of Eliezer, who was of Jorim, who was of Mathat, who was of Levi,

vv. 21–38

Our Lord comes to baptism to show His approval of St John, and also to sanctify water itself, so that it may be used in the sacrament of baptism. The *heaven was opened* to show that heaven is made accessible to the members of His mystical body when they receive this sacrament.

God the Father spoke from heaven when His *beloved Son* was baptised. He is accustomed, so to speak, to give some sign of approval when any new venture is undertaken with which He is *well pleased*. Thus, St Benedict, St Dominic and other founders have worked miracles as a sign that the manner of life that they were instituting was pleasing to God.

It is supposed that St Luke gives the legal genealogy of our Lord. This differs from the physical genealogy, because of the 'levirate' law, by which a younger brother would marry the childless widow of his elder brother, to whom the younger brother's offspring would be reckoned. But in both respects, St Joseph was of the line of *David*.

In accordance with his promise, *to write in order, having diligently attained to all things from the beginning,* St Luke traces the

30 Who was of Simeon, who was of Judas, who was of Joseph, who was of Jona, who was of Eliakim,

31 Who was of Melea, who was of Menna, who was of Mathatha, who was of Nathan, who was of David,

32 Who was of Jesse, who was of Obed, who was of Booz, who was of Salmon, who was of Naasson,

33 Who was of Aminadab, who was of Aram, who was of Esron, who was of Phares, who was of Judas,

34 Who was of Jacob, who was of Isaac, who was of Abraham, who was of Thare, who was of Nachor,

35 Who was of Sarug, who was of Ragau, who was of Phaleg, who was of Heber, who was of Sale,

36 Who was of Cainan, who was of Arphaxad, who was of Sem, who was of Noe, who was of Lamech,

37 Who was of Mathusale, who was of Henoch, who was of Jared, who was of Malaleel, who was of Cainan,

38 Who was of Henos, who was of Seth, who was of Adam, who was of God.

genealogy of Jesus the new Adam all the way to the first Adam, *who was of God.* Seventy-seven names occur in it. The symbolic meaning of the number is said to come from its components: eleven is the biblical number of transgression, since it goes beyond the ten of the commandments, while seven is the number of fullness. By His baptism, the Lord takes all the transgressions of mankind upon Himself.

The Church sings the genealogy of St Luke on the feast of the Epiphany, after the last responsory at Matins.[1]

---

1 In some dioceses it is also customary to sing it on the following Sunday, before High Mass.

1 And Jesus being full of the Holy Ghost, returned from the Jordan, and was led by the Spirit into the desert,

2 For the space of forty days; and was tempted by the devil. And he ate nothing in those days; and when they were ended, he was hungry.

3 And the devil said to him: If thou be the Son of God, say to this stone that it be made bread.

4 And Jesus answered him: It is written, that Man liveth not by bread alone, but by every word of God.

5 And the devil led him into a high mountain, and shewed him all the kingdoms of the world in a moment of time;

6 And he said to him: To thee will I give all this power, and the glory of them; for to me they are delivered, and to whom I will, I give them.

7 If thou therefore wilt adore before me, all shall be thine.

8 And Jesus answering said to him: It is written: Thou shalt adore the Lord thy God, and him only shalt thou serve.

9 And he brought him to Jerusalem, and set him on a pinnacle of the temple, and he said to him: If thou be the Son of God, cast thyself from hence.

10 For it is written, that He hath given his angels charge over thee, that they keep thee.

11 And that in their hands they shall bear thee up, lest perhaps thou dash thy foot against a stone.

12 And Jesus answering, said to him: It is said: Thou shalt not tempt the Lord thy God.

13 And all the temptation being ended, the devil departed from him for a time.

VV. 1–13

ITH US, FASTING SERVES THREE PUR-
poses: it weakens concupiscence; it helps us pray with
more devotion; and it serves to expiate sin. The first
two of these motives for fasting did not apply to our Lord. It
was the third that moved Him to perform this great fast in the
desert, since it was not during His passion only that He made
reparation for the sins of the world.

The devil appears, presumably under the form of a holy angel.
Why did Christ allow the devil to test Him? It was so that God's
victory over the devil would be more glorious, in that the enemy
had enjoyed full scope to obstruct man's salvation. Christ also
wished to show us that He is the new Adam, who undid the evil
which the first Adam introduced into the world when he was
overcome by the serpent, and turned the garden into a desert.

The devil has observed, as best he can, the life of our Lord,
and he perhaps suspects that Jesus is the incarnate Son, since
he has been unable to find any sin in Him; yet at the same
time his pride makes it incredible to him that God should have
entered the world in so humble and inconspicuous a way. So,
he is perplexed: the point of the temptations is to find out who
this Man is. If the devil can cause Him to sin, that will show at
least that He is not God incarnate.

But our Lord is not going to give away His identity to the
enemy. That would risk obstructing the redemption. *None of the
princes of this world,* that is, the fallen spirits, *would have crucified
the Lord of glory*, had they recognised the wisdom of God. So while
He remains sinless, He also conceals His authority. In replying
to Satan, Christ is content to quote three times from the Book
of Deuteronomy, as any pious Jew might have done.

Yet in another, veiled way, He does tell the devil what the
latter wants to know; but the devil will realise this only later,
for his greater humiliation. The devil bids Christ turn a *stone* into
bread, to satisfy His hunger. The Lord replies: *Man does not live by*

14 And Jesus returned in the power of the spirit, into Galilee, and the fame of him went out through the whole country.

15 And he taught in their synagogues, and was magnified by all.

16 And he came to Nazareth, where he was brought up: and he went into the

bread alone, but by every word of God. On the surface, this is simply a reminder that eternal life is greater than temporal, and hence that He would command the stone only if God had revealed that He ought to work this miracle. The hidden meaning may be: "If every word of God brings life to a man, how much more can the eternal Word of God, who I am, sustain the life of the man whom you see, without need for a further miracle." Christ thus tells the devil of His divinity, which is the very thing he wanted to know; and yet he does not grasp it.

It is the same with the second and third temptations mentioned by St Luke. When the devil bids Christ fall down before him in worship, and to jump from the parapet of the temple, He replies, *Thou shalt adore the Lord thy God* and *Thou shalt not tempt the Lord thy God.* On the surface, Jesus is speaking of His own obligations as a Jew born under the Law; beneath this, He is rebuking the devil for sinning against *his* creaturely obligations toward his Creator, come in the flesh.

St Matthew places third the temptation to acquire all the kingdoms of the world, and this seems to have been the historical order, since it is at this temptation that the Lord commands the devil to depart, thus vindicating His Father's honour, which the devil here violates so openly. Why then does St Luke, who has undertaken at the start of his gospel to write *in order*, reverse the second and third temptations? It is hard to be sure. Perhaps he wishes to show us that some people who resist temptations to rank and power are still susceptible to vain glory, wishing to be admired by others. This reminder is especially relevant for preachers: and since our Lord is now to begin His preaching, the Holy Spirit inspired the evangelist to show Christ as the model for those who will assume this office.

vv. 14–30

Why were *the eyes of all in the synagogue fixed on him*? No doubt, because they had heard of the *great things* that He had *done in Caphernaum*; and also, perhaps, because of the beauty of His reading, or chanting, of the words of Isaias. But their admiration is superficial and soon dissipates, when Christ intimates

synagogue, according to his custom, on the sabbath day; and he rose up to read.

17 And the book of Isaias the prophet was delivered unto him. And as he unfolded the book, he found the place where it was written:

18 The Spirit of the Lord is upon me. Wherefore he hath anointed me to preach the gospel to the poor, he hath sent me to heal the contrite of heart,

19 To preach deliverance to the captives, and sight to the blind, to set at liberty them that are bruised, to preach the acceptable year of the Lord, and the day of reward.

20 And when he had folded the book, he restored it to the minister, and sat down. And the eyes of all in the synagogue were fixed on him.

21 And he began to say to them: This day is fulfilled this scripture in your ears.

22 And all gave testimony to him: and they wondered at the words of grace that proceeded from his mouth, and they said: Is not this the son of Joseph?

23 And he said to them: Doubtless you will say to me this

similitude: Physician, heal thyself: as great things as we have heard done in Capharnaum, do also here in thy own country.

24 And he said: Amen I say to you, that no prophet is accepted in his own country.

25 In truth I say to you, there were many widows in the days of Elias in Israel, when heaven was shut up three years and six months, when there was a great famine throughout all the earth.

26 And to none of them was Elias sent, but to Sarepta of Sidon, to a widow woman.

27 And there were many lepers in Israel in the time of Eliseus the prophet: and none of them was cleansed but Naaman the Syrian.

28 And all they in the synagogue, hearing these things, were filled with anger.

29 And they rose up and thrust him out of the city; and they brought him to the brow of the hill, whereon their city was built, that they might cast him down headlong.

30 But he passing through the midst of them, went his way.

that in *the acceptable year,* that is, the time of the new covenant, fleshly ties will not suffice to make a person into one of God's chosen. For He speaks of His future Church under the figure of a foreign widow, miraculously saved from starvation, and a foreign leper, miraculously made clean by water.

On hearing the gospel for the first time, the synagogue seeks to put Him to death. By divine power He takes away their own ability to act, and they apparently remain rooted to the spot while He returns from *the brow of the cliff.* Imitating this, rulers within Christendom have used their power to restrain those who would hinder the preaching of the word, or who would corrupt it.

Christ's rejection by the influential men of Nazareth foreshadows His rejection by the rulers of all the Jews: *he came to his own and his own received him not.* From this will come *a great famine* of hearing the word of God *throughout all the land* of Israel.

31 And he went down into Capharnaum, a city of Galilee,
and there he taught them
on the sabbath days.

32 And they were astonished at
his doctrine: for his speech
was with power.

33 And in the synagogue there
was a man who had an un-
clean devil, and he cried out
with a loud voice,

34 Saying: Let us alone, what
have we to do with thee, Jesus of Nazareth? art thou
come to destroy us? I know
thee who thou art, the holy
one of God.

35 And Jesus rebuked him, saying: Hold thy peace, and go
out of him. And when the
devil had thrown him into
the midst, he went out of
him, and hurt him not at all.

36 And there came fear upon
all, and they talked among
themselves, saying: What
word is this, for with authority and power he com-
mandeth the unclean spirits,
and they go out?

37 And the fame of him was
published into every place
of the country.

38 And Jesus rising up out of
the synagogue, went into
Simon's house. And Si-
mon's wife's mother was
taken with a great fever, and
they besought him for her.

39 And standing over her, he
commanded the fever, and
it left her. And immediately rising, she ministered to
them.

40 And when the sun was
down, all they that had any
sick with diverse diseases,
brought them to him. But
he laying his hands on every
one of them, healed them.

41 And devils went out from
many, crying out and say-
ing: Thou art the Son of
God. And rebuking them he
suffered them not to speak,
for they knew that he was
Christ.

42 And when it was day, going
out he went into a desert
place, and the multitudes
sought him, and came unto
him: and they stayed him
that he should not depart
from them.

43 To whom he said: To other
cities also I must preach the
kingdom of God: for therefore am I sent.

44 And he was preaching in the
synagogues of Galilee.

vv. 31–44

In Capharnaum, the man possessed by the unclean spirit says *I know who you are, the holy one of God.* The devil is lying: he does not know who Christ is, but rather is trying to provoke Him to reveal it, one way or the other. Our Lord silences him both because He does not wish to make known His identity to the demons, and also because He does not wish to receive testimony from them.

Does the demon at least know that Jesus is the Messias, even though not whether He is God? It is possible, but it is also possible that he knows, from the Old Testament, or from the knowledge given to him at his creation, that the Messias will be God, and hence that he is ignorant of both these attributes of Christ. If so, we should translate a later verse in this chapter differently. Instead of reading it as: *He would not allow them to speak, for they knew that he was Christ,* we should translate: "He would not allow them to say that they knew that he was Christ".

Simon's wife's mother. We do not know whether his wife was still living. If she was, they will soon separate for the sake of the gospel by mutual consent, if they have not already done so, since elsewhere Peter says: *We have left all things and have followed thee,* and our Lord in his reply includes a *wife* in His enumeration of the persons who are left when someone becomes an apostle (Matt. 19).

Though He could have cured all the sick simultaneously, and with a word, or with a simple act of the will, Christ prefers to cure them by *laying his hands on every one of them,* both to show His love for each one, by a natural human gesture, and to show that His body is divine, since it is assumed into the Person of the Word. He is also foreshadowing the sacrament of the Church, where He heals souls through bodily instruments, one at a time.

1 And it came to pass, that when the multitudes pressed upon him to hear the word of God, he stood by the lake of Genesareth,

2 And saw two ships standing by the lake: but the fishermen were gone out of them, and were washing their nets.

3 And going into one of the ships that was Simon's, he desired him to draw back a little from the land. And sitting he taught the multitudes out of the ship.

4 Now when he had ceased to speak, he said to Simon: Launch out into the deep, and let down your nets for a draught.

5 And Simon answering said to him: Master, we have labored all the night, and have taken nothing: but at thy word I will let down the net.

6 And when they had done this, they enclosed a very great multitude of fishes, and their net broke.

7 And they beckoned to their partners that were in the other ship, that they should come and help them. And they came, and filled both the ships, so that they were almost sinking.

8 Which when Simon Peter saw, he fell down at Jesus' knees, saying: Depart from me, for I am a sinful man, O Lord.

9 For he was wholly astonished, and all that were with him, at the draught of the fishes which they had taken.

10 And so were also James and John the sons of Zebedee, who were Simon's partners. And Jesus saith to Simon: Fear not: from henceforth thou shalt catch men.

11 And having brought their ships to land, leaving all things, they followed him.

12 And it came to pass, when he was in a certain city, behold a man full of leprosy, who seeing Jesus, and falling on his face, besought him, saying: Lord, if thou wilt, thou canst make me clean.

13 And stretching forth his hand, he touched him, saying: I will. Be thou cleansed. And immediately the leprosy departed from him.

14 And he charged him that he should tell no man, but, Go,

vv. 1–11

NETS CAN BE A SYMBOL FOR SPEECHES. AS a net is carefully fashioned from many cords, so a speech, for example a political or philosophical discourse, is woven from many words. By the miraculous draught of fish, our Lord enacts a parable for the benefit of the apostles, by whose words the world is to be converted. First, they *laboured all the night,* catching *nothing.* In this they may represent all those who, lacking Christ's commission, try in vain to persuade men to reform their lives and master their passions, for example the philosophers who preached and taught unsuccessfully during the night of paganism. But Christ comes to preach, and so now the fishermen wash their nets, since He appointed preachers of a better philosophy, and taught them to purify their words. After that, He enters Simon's boat, since, risen from the dead He will appoint St Peter as head of the Church on earth, and then, by His Ascension, draw *back a little from the land*.

Now the preaching is successful, since after Pentecost a multitude is converted. But why are there two ships? Perhaps because Peter was in a special way the apostle *to the circumcised*, and so the other ship represents the churches of the gentiles. Yet there is but one net, Peter's, resting on both ships, since converted Jews and converted Gentiles are members of the same Church. They were *almost sinking,* because sometimes the very multitude of the faithful proves a danger to the Church, when there are scarcely enough good bishops and priests to govern and instruct them.

vv. 12–16

Next, the Lord heals a man. With his physician's eye, St Luke does not simply call the man a leper, as do St Matthew and St Mark, but specifies that he was *full of leprosy.* Our Lord touches him. It was not forbidden to touch lepers, but it made the one who did so ritually unclean until he had purified himself. But Christ does not become ritually unclean, since at the

shew thyself to the priest, and offer for thy cleansing according as Moses commanded, for a testimony to them.

15 But the fame of him went abroad the more, and great multitudes came together to hear, and to be healed by him of their infirmities.

16 And he retired into the desert, and prayed.

17 And it came to pass on a certain day, as he sat teaching, that there were also Pharisees and doctors of the law sitting by, that were come out of every town of Galilee, and Judea and Jerusalem: and the power of the Lord was to heal them.

18 And behold, men brought in a bed a man, who had the palsy: and they sought means to bring him in, and to lay him before him.

19 And when they could not find by what way they might bring him in, because of the multitude, they went up upon the roof, and let him down through the tiles with his bed into the midst before Jesus.

20 Whose faith when he saw, he said: Man, thy sins are forgiven thee.

21 And the scribes and Pharisees began to think, saying: Who is this who speaketh blasphemies? Who can forgive sins, but God alone?

22 And when Jesus knew their thoughts, answering, he said to them: What is it you think in your hearts?

23 Which is easier to say, Thy sins are forgiven thee; or to say, Arise and walk?

24 But that you may know that the Son of man hath power on earth to forgive sins, (he saith to the sick of the palsy,) I say to thee, Arise, take up thy bed, and go into thy house.

moment of touching him, *the leprosy departed*.

Since the old Law was still in force for the Jews, He tells the man to perform the sacrifice which Leviticus required of lepers who had been cured. This was not a small thing: even the poor had to provide a lamb, two doves and two sparrows, while the rich had to replace the doves with a second lamb and an ewe. The ceremony by which they were offered was long and complex, with the former leper having also to be anointed with blood and oil; only when it was done was the man allowed to enter the holy city. It symbolised the sacrifices and sacraments of the new Law, by which a Christian, though already cleansed of original sin, must enter heaven.

When our Lord's *fame went abroad the more*, He *retired into the desert*. It is done as a lesson to preachers to rely more on prayer than on fame for the spreading of the faith.

vv. 17–32

Generally, when Christ heals a person miraculously, He requires faith from the one cured. Here, nothing is said about the faith of the *man who had the palsy*; rather, Christ heals him when he sees *their faith*, that is, the stretcher-bearers'. This encourages us to bring to Him, at least by our prayers, those who are without faith and thus paralysed as far as the spiritual life is concerned. But to our prayers we may have to add penances in order to succeed, as it were doing violence to the clay of our bodies, as these men had to take away something from the clay of the *roof*.

Jesus forgives his sins before curing him, partly to show the relative importance of soul and body, and partly to show that our sins can induce God to withhold even temporal blessings from us.

Why does He ask the scribes and Pharisees: *Which is easier to say?* They were thinking within themselves that it was easy to claim to forgive sins, since, as they imagined, there was no way to test the claim. He corrects them: not only is forgiving sins in itself a greater work than restoring the use of a man's limbs — greater, said St Augustine, than creating the heavens and the earth — but there is also a way to test it. Anyone who can truly absolve in his own name can also work a bodily cure, which Christ therefore goes on to perform.

25 And immediately rising up before them, he took up the bed on which he lay; and he went away to his own house, glorifying God.

26 And all were astonished; and they glorified God. And they were filled with fear, saying: We have seen wonderful things today.

27 And after these things he went forth, and saw a publican named Levi, sitting at the receipt of custom, and he said to him: Follow me.

28 And leaving all things, he rose up and followed him.

29 And Levi made him a great feast in his own house; and there was a great company of publicans, and of others, that were at table with them.

30 But the Pharisees and scribes murmured, saying to his disciples: Why do you eat and drink with publicans and sinners?

31 And Jesus answering, said to them: They that are whole, need not the physician: but they that are sick.

32 I came not to call the just, but sinners to penance.

33 And they said to him: Why do the disciples of John fast often, and make prayers, and the disciples of the Pharisees in like manner; but thine eat and drink?

34 To whom he said: Can you make the children of the bridegroom fast, whilst the bridegroom is with them?

35 But the days will come, when the bridegroom shall be taken away from them, then shall they fast in those days.

vv. 32–39

Christ *came not to call the just*, because He came to call men not angels. Since he came *to call sinners to penance*, He came for all men, the Pharisees and scribes included. St Thomas Aquinas remarks that while He was them, the apostles could freely dine with *publicans and sinners*, since His very presence prevented them from being unduly influenced by these latter, but that since His Ascension, when *the bridegroom* was *taken away from them*, Christ's disciples have had to be more circumspect.

The Lord does not allude to the implication that His disciples did not *make prayers*, presumably because it was untrue, and could be easily known to be so.

Since the disciples of St John the Baptist and the disciples of the Pharisees, in different ways and for different motives, were fasting so as to be able to practice the old Law more perfectly, and since it was His presence, as the preacher of the gospel of grace, which prevents His own disciples from fasting beyond what was compulsory for all Jews, our Lord now speaks of the relation of the old to the new.

36 And he spoke also a similitude to them: That no man putteth a piece from a new garment upon an old garment; otherwise he both rendeth the new, and the piece taken from the new agreeth not with the old.

37 And no man putteth new wine into an old bottle: otherwise the new wine will break the bottles, and it will be spilled, and the bottles will be lost.

38 But new wine must be put into new bottles; and both are preserved.

39 And no man drinking old, hath presently a mind to new: for he saith, The old is better.

It would be a strange person who cut up a *new garment* in order to patch up an *old* one. It would be equally incongruous to continue to practice Judaism while embellishing it with some parts of the gospel, for example with the belief that Jesus is the Messias and with baptism in His name. Such a person *rendeth the new* covenant, by separating belief in Christ from the gospel's teaching that for those who believe, *there is neither Gentile nor Jew.* And the part of the gospel that such a person adopts *agreeth not with the old* covenant, since this latter speaks of Christ as still to come, not as having already suffered. Thus, to eat the passover meal, which was instituted as a figure, is not possible for those who know that the true Lamb has now been slain.

The second image, *new wine* continuing to ferment within *old bottles* or skins, intensifies the message. On Pentecost, the Church was filled with the grace of the Holy Ghost as with new wine. If a Christian returns to the practice of the old Law, he sins mortally and thus this wine is *spilled*. But he also bursts the old skins: for the old Law can serve no purpose for him, who has rejected the One of whom it speaks. What then are the *new bottles*? The sacraments and ceremonies of the Church.

Yet our Lord knows that many of the people of Israel, even if they glimpse the beauty of His teaching, will find it too hard to give up their ancestral ways. They will say, *the old* Law *is better.*

CHAPTER 6

1 And it came to pass on the second first sabbath, that as he went through the corn fields, his disciples plucked the ears, and did eat, rubbing them in their hands.

2 And some of the Pharisees said to them: Why do you that which is not lawful on the sabbath days?

3 And Jesus answering them, said: Have you not read so much as this, what David did, when himself was hungry, and they that were with him:

4 How he went into the house of God, and took and ate the bread of proposition, and gave to them that were with him, which is not lawful to eat but only for the priests?

5 And he said to them: The Son of man is Lord also of the sabbath.

6 And it came to pass also on another sabbath, that he entered into the synagogue, and taught. And there was a man, whose right hand was withered.

7 And the scribes and Pharisees watched if he would heal on the sabbath; that they might find an accusation against him.

8 But he knew their thoughts; and said to the man who had the withered hand: Arise and stand forth in the midst. And rising he stood forth.

9 Then Jesus said to them: I ask you, if it be lawful on the sabbath days to do good, or to do evil; to save life, or to destroy?

10 And looking round about on them all, he said to the man: Stretch forth thy hand. And he stretched it forth: and his hand was restored.

11 And they were filled with madness; and they talked one with another, what they might do to Jesus.

12 And it came to pass in those days, that he went out into a mountain to pray, and he passed the whole night in the prayer of God.

13 And when day was come, he called unto him his disciples; and he chose twelve of them (whom also he named apostles):

VV. 1–11

THE SECOND FIRST SABBATH. 'SECOND FIRST' is the literal translation of a Greek word whose significance is no longer known. It may refer to the first Sabbath after the second day of the Passover.

The old Law forbade farmers to reap their fields to the edge, so that something would be left for the poor and for wayfarers, and the apostles make use of this law. Christ argues *a fortiori*: if *David* and his men, to avoid fainting on their journey, could be so far dispensed from the provisions of the Law as to eat the holy *bread*, how much more can the followers of the true David be dispensed so as to take common *corn*. But lest the Pharisees think of Him as only a rabbi, arguing to a conclusion by an analogy, He indicates that He has a unique right to interpret the scope of the Sabbath Law, and even to dispense from it, being *Lord of the Sabbath*.

Neither in the corn fields nor in the synagogue did Christ break the Sabbath. Rather, He rejected the excessively strict, even superstitious, interpretation of the Pharisees. Since the Sabbath was given that the Jews might delight in serving God, the giver of life, it is impossible to break the Sabbath by preserving or restoring life, or in general by doing deeds that evidently redound to God's glory. He gives the Pharisees the opportunity to consider this principle, but instead, they immediately break the Law themselves by plotting to destroy human life, *filled with madness* and talking *one with another, what they might do to Jesus*.

v. 12–16

Christ's prayer is called *the prayer of God*, since as well as being made to God the Father, it is itself divine. From St John we learn that Christ *knew from the first who he was that would betray him*. Yet He does not choose Judas in order that Judas may become a traitor. He chooses the twelve according to their present

14 Simon, whom he surnamed Peter, and Andrew his brother, James and John, Philip and Bartholomew,

15 Matthew and Thomas, James the son of Alpheus,

and Simon who is called Zelotes,

16 And Jude, the brother of James, and Judas Iscariot, who was the traitor.

17 And coming down with them, he stood in a plain place, and the company of his disciples, and a very great multitude of people from all Judea and Jerusalem, and the sea coast both of Tyre and Sidon,

18 Who were come to hear him, and to be healed of their diseases. And they that were troubled with unclean spirits, were cured.

19 And all the multitude sought to touch him, for virtue went out from him, and healed all.

20 And he, lifting up his eyes on his disciples, said: Blessed are ye poor, for yours is the kingdom of God.

21 Blessed are ye that hunger now: for you shall be filled. Blessed are ye that weep now: for you shall laugh.

22 Blessed shall you be when men shall hate you, and when they shall separate you, and shall reproach you, and cast out your name as evil, for the Son of man's sake.

23 Be glad in that day and rejoice; for behold, your reward is great in heaven. For according to these things did their fathers to the prophets.

24 But woe to you that are rich: for you have your consolation.

25 Woe to you that are filled: for you shall hunger. Woe to you that now laugh: for you shall mourn and weep.

26 Woe to you when men shall bless you: for according to these things did their fathers to the false prophets.

27 But I say to you that hear: Love your enemies, do good to them that hate you.

28 Bless them that curse you, and pray for them that calumniate you.

29 And to him that striketh thee on the one cheek, offer

dispositions, because these are the men currently most apt for the apostolate. One analogy for Christ's prophetic knowledge may be the knowledge which a bishop or parish priest has under the seal of the confessional, but which he cannot make use of in order to govern his flock.

vv. 17–26

These beatitudes appear to have been spoken on a different occasion from those recorded by St Matthew. It would hardly be surprising for the Lord to give the same teaching to different listeners, or even to the same listeners on a different occasion, varying slightly the words.

Christ seems here to fulfil the prophecy of our Lady in the *Magnificat*, and to abrogate the clause of the old covenant by which obedience to the Law would result in temporal well-being. Under the new covenant, God will still sometimes reward and punish human acts in this life, lest men begin to doubt His justice. But whereas hitherto, the friends of God had to remain in *Sheol* after their death, where the very delay of beatitude could serve to expiate their faults, His friends now have the prospect of heaven immediately after death, and so God wishes them to expiate their faults in this life. For this reason, and so that they more closely resemble their King, He will from now on often allow the spontaneous conspiracy of the worldly against the just to succeed. Thus, for the followers of Christ whose consciences do not condemn them, the very fact of poverty, *hunger*, sorrows or scorn will serve to strengthen their hope in the closeness of the heavenly *reward*, whereas unbroken prosperity will from now on be a sign of reprobation.

vv. 27–38

The words of Christ can always be followed, either in literal fact or in preparedness of spirit. If we have only ourselves to please then we can allow ourselves literally to be despoiled of our *goods*. If we have also to protect the rights of others, as the

also the other. And him that taketh away from thee thy cloak, forbid not to take thy coat also.

30 Give to every one that asketh thee, and of him that taketh away thy goods, ask them not again.

31 And as you would that men should do to you, do you also to them in like manner.

32 And if you love them that love you, what thanks are to you? for sinners also love those that love them.

33 And if you do good to them who do good to you, what thanks are to you? for sinners also do this.

34 And if you lend to them of whom you hope to receive, what thanks are to you? for sinners also lend to sinners, for to receive as much.

35 But love ye your enemies: do good, and lend, hoping for nothing thereby: and your reward shall be great, and you shall be the sons of the Highest; for he is kind to the unthankful, and to the evil.

36 Be ye therefore merciful, as your Father also is merciful.

37 Judge not, and you shall not be judged. Condemn not, and you shall not be condemned. Forgive, and you shall be forgiven.

38 Give, and it shall be given to you: good measure and pressed down and shaken together and running over shall they give into your bosom. For with the same measure that you shall mete withal, it shall be measured to you again.

39 And he spoke also to them a similitude: Can the blind lead the blind? do they not both fall into the ditch?

40 The disciple is not above his master: but every one shall be perfect, if he be as his master.

41 And why seest thou the mote in thy brother's eye: but the beam that is in thy own eye thou considerest not?

42 Or how canst thou say to thy brother: Brother, let me pull the mote out of thy eye, when thou thyself seest not the beam in thy own eye?

father of a family or the ruler of a nation, then we must resist the evil-doer for the sake of these others, while maintaining the readiness to forsake our goods should our responsibilities pass away.

Is it true that sinners also *do good* to those who do good to them? Yes, by a kind of natural love, especially to those whom they like or to those of their own family or nation. Such love is not false in itself, but it can co-exist with a love of oneself above all things even to the contempt of God. But love of one's *enemies* is beyond the power of nature.

What is the difference between judging and condemning? I seem to *judge* when I ascribe to myself, even silently, an authority over another man that entitles me to punish him for his spiritual state; I *condemn* when I declare, even internally, that this or that person will surely go to hell, or ought to do so. If the faithful can refrain from doing these things, Christ will not use His authority to punish them or condemn them to hell.

Who are *they* who *will give into the bosom* of the man who gives, and what do they give? Perhaps it is the three divine Persons, who give Themselves. By acting generously, while in a state of grace, we can merit a new coming of the Blessed Trinity to our soul. The paradox of the infinite Creator dwelling within His finite creature is expressed by the words, *good measure, pressed down, shaken together, running over.* And to the *measure* or degree of charity with which we govern our lives will correspond the degree of beatitude that *shall be measured to* us *again* when those lives are over.

vv. 39–49

Having spoken of what pertains to His followers in general, our Lord now addresses those in the Church who will teach others. The first requirement of a Christian teacher is that he be not *blind,* that is, lacking supernatural faith. Those who direct themselves according to the teaching of such a one must inevitably *fall into the ditch* after death.

But right faith is not sufficient to make someone a good teacher. He needs also to be free from passions if he is to *be as his master,* Christ. The *hypocrite* is not necessarily a man who is

Hypocrite, cast first the beam out of thy own eye; and then shalt thou see clearly to take out the mote from thy brother's eye.

43 For there is no good tree that bringeth forth evil fruit; nor an evil tree that bringeth forth good fruit.

44 For every tree is known by its fruit. For men do not gather figs from thorns; nor from a bramble bush do they gather the grape.

45 A good man out of the good treasure of his heart bringeth forth that which is good: and an evil man out of the evil treasure bringeth forth that which is evil. For out of the abundance of the heart the mouth speaketh.

46 And why call you me, Lord, Lord; and do not the things which I say?

47 Every one that cometh to me, and heareth my words, and doth them, I will shew you to whom he is like.

48 He is like to a man building a house, who digged deep, and laid the foundation upon a rock. And when a flood came, the stream beat vehemently upon that house, and it could not shake it; for it was founded on a rock.

49 But he that heareth, and doth not, is like to a man building his house upon the earth without a foundation: against which the stream beat vehemently, and immediately it fell, and the ruin of that house was great.

playing a part with the fully conscious intention of deceiving others. He is more commonly someone who, under the sway of some powerful passion such as vain glory or resentment, deceives himself about his own motivations. Until this passion, strong as a *beam*, is removed from our mind's *eye*, we will seek to gratify it, even without fully realising the fact, in our dealings with others.

Next, Christ seems to address those who will be torn between disparate teachers, since He foresees, as St Paul also would predict, that *ravening wolves will enter in, not sparing of the flock* (Acts 20). First, we are to assess the *tree* by the *fruits*, that is, the teacher by his life and speech. To the extent that these fruits correspond to what we already know of God's word, this teacher enjoys a greater presumption of reliability when it comes to doubtful matters.

But the trees may also stand for different religions and philosophies of life. When the teaching of the Catholic religion and that of some other religion or philosophy differ, then a person will find that the former teaching assists him to grow in holiness, while the latter obstruct this. For example, the teaching that images of the saints should be venerated serves to remind us of the existence of the saints and to encourage us to imitate them. Or again, the teaching that the state of justification can be lost makes us more diligent about conforming ourselves to the will of God. These are good fruits, which is a sign that the religion that produces them comes from God, and not from the imaginations of fallen men, signified by the *thorns* and *bramble bush* that original sin brought into the world.

The two men may be taken to refer to Christ and the devil, or to Christ and antichrist. Our Lord first *brought forth* the *good treasure* of the gospel from His sacred *heart*. Then, in order to build the *house* of the Church, He *digged deep* until He reached the rock: in humility He reached the lowest place, and there built the Church upon Himself, since *the rock was Christ*. The *stream* of this present life, which flows rapidly until the end of the world, will *beat upon* the Church but not *shake* it.

The other man builds *upon the earth,* since the devil relies on the earthly motivations of men to erect his unstable kingdom. It will fall *immediately* that history has run its course.

1 And when he had finished all his words in the hearing of the people, he entered into Capharnaum.

2 And the servant of a certain centurion, who was dear to him, being sick, was ready to die.

3 And when he had heard of Jesus, he sent unto him the ancients of the Jews, desiring him to come and heal his servant.

4 And when they came to Jesus, they besought him earnestly, saying to him: He is worthy that thou shouldest do this for him.

5 For he loveth our nation; and he hath built us a synagogue.

6 And Jesus went with them. And when he was now not far from the house, the centurion sent his friends to him, saying: Lord, trouble not thyself; for I am not worthy that thou shouldest enter under my roof.

7 For which cause neither did I think myself worthy to come to thee; but say the word, and my servant shall be healed.

8 For I also am a man subject to authority, having under me soldiers: and I say to one, Go, and he goeth; and to another, Come, and he cometh; and to my servant, Do this, and he doth it.

9 Which Jesus hearing, marvelled: and turning about to the multitude that followed him, he said: Amen I say to you, I have not found so great faith, not even in Israel.

10 And they who were sent, being returned to the house, found the servant whole who had been sick.

VV. 1–10

PEOPLE SOMETIMES ASK: "HOW WAS IT POS-sible for our Lord to be surprised by anything that happened? Since He is God, He knew everything in advance!" Others sometimes reply to this by saying that He knew everything in His divine nature, not His human nature, and so in His human nature He could be surprised.

But that answer is insufficient, since in His human nature also, Christ knew, not least by the beatific vision which He enjoyed from the first moment of the creation of His soul, all that had happened or would happen. Yet He could feel wonder, or surprise, when He learned, in the ordinary human way in which men learn things, something which was out of the ordinary run of events, even though it was something that He knew already in another, higher way. There are analogies for this in our own experience: we can know something in one way and still feel wonder when we come to learn it in another. I may know that a friend of mine has married or entered a religious order, and still find it strange to see him for the first time with his wife, or wearing his religious habit.

It was in this way that our Lord *marvelled* at the faith of the centurion. It was not unknown for gentiles to become convinced of the election of Israel, and to associate themselves to the people of God as, so to speak, auxiliary members. But for a gentile to have so pure a faith that he shrank from receiving Christ into his home, or even from meeting Him, while still maintaining utter confidence that Christ need but *say the word* and his servant, *ready to die*, would be restored to health — that was something marvellous. It must have been refreshing for our Lord to hear it.

By humbly sending friends to speak for him rather than venturing to come himself, the centurion merits the grace of surpassing in faith all those whom Christ has *found in Israel*. Yet how is this, since certainly the Blessed Virgin far surpassed the

11 And it came to pass afterwards, that he went into a city that is called Naim; and there went with him his disciples, and a great multitude.

12 And when he came nigh to the gate of the city, behold a dead man was carried out, the only son of his mother; and she was a widow: and a great multitude of the city was with her.

13 Whom when the Lord had seen, being moved with mercy towards her, he said to her: Weep not.

centurion in faith, and since St Joseph and St John the Baptist must have done so also? Perhaps He means those who represent Israel officially, as this centurion was a representative of the Roman empire. Nicodemus and Joseph of Arimathea, for example, dared not confess Him openly.

By his faith, the centurion seems to see a certain similarity between himself and Jesus. He recognises Christ as the Son who, in His humanity, is *subject to* the Father's *authority*, and who therefore *goeth and cometh* as the Father wills. He seems also to discern the future multitude of disciples, to be made *soldiers* of Christ by the sacrament of confirmation.

Jesus could have gone to see the centurion, but that might have appeared like seeking for praise, after the centurion's confession of His power. The Lord did not refuse tokens of veneration, indeed of adoration, during His life on earth; but He does not receive them openly before a crowd who do not all have faith, lest this turn to their harm. By His way of working the miracle, He also symbolises how He will heal the gentile nations at a distance, through the preaching of the apostles, after His ascension.

The centurion had honoured the true religion and the nation of Israel when he *built a synagogue* in Capharnaum. God will reward and honour him by using his words as a part of the religion of the new Israel. Throughout the world, priests will say like the centurion, and the faithful with them, *Lord, I am not worthy that thou shouldest enter under my roof.*

Symbolically, the fact that this Roman officer built the synagogue in Simon Peter's town, intimates that the Roman imperial power will in due time become the chief temporal protector of religion within the Church, as it were, St Peter's new city.

VV. 11–17

This miracle at Naim is another miniature of the redemption. Two crowds confront each other. Christ approaches the city accompanied by *his disciples and a great multitude*. The widow is leaving it with her dead son, *and a great multitude was with her.* Likewise, when the Son came into the world, says St Paul, the Father declared: *Let all the angels of God adore him*, which was

14 And he came near and touched the bier. And they that carried it, stood still. And he said: Young man, I say to thee, arise.

15 And he that was dead, sat up, and began to speak. And he gave him to his mother.

16 And there came a fear on them all: and they glorified God, saying: A great prophet is risen up among us: and, God hath visited his people.

17 And this rumour of him went forth throughout all Judea, and throughout all the country round about.

18 And John's disciples told him of all these things.

19 And John called to him two of his disciples, and sent them to Jesus, saying: Art thou he that art to come; or look we for another?

20 And when the men were come unto him, they said: John the Baptist hath sent us to thee, saying: Art thou he that art to come; or look we for another?

21 (And in that same hour, he cured many of their diseases, and hurts, and evil spirits: and to many that were blind he gave sight.)

22 And answering, he said to them: Go and relate to John what you have heard and seen: the blind see, the lame walk, the lepers are made clean, the deaf hear, the dead rise again, to the poor the gospel is preached:

23 And blessed is he whosoever shall not be scandalized in me.

certainly a great host. He found man, the only offspring of Eve, dead by reason of sin, as it were being carried out of the world, destined for Sheol, surrounded by fallen spirits gloating over him. Jesus stretched out His hand to the wood and the bearers stood still, since by embracing the Cross, He disarmed the principalities and powers. He dried the tears of Eve in hell, raised up her offspring and *gave him to his mother*.

Perhaps He was also *moved with mercy* by the resemblance which this unnamed woman bore to His own mother. She too was a widow; she too would soon lose her *only son*. The widow of Naim thus represents the Blessed Virgin, standing by the Cross of Christ. Mary knew the prophecies; she knew that Isaias had foretold that the Messias would be rejected and become Himself an offering for sin. When she replied to the angel's message, *Be it done to me according to thy word*, she knew therefore that she was providing a Victim for the great sacrifice. On Calvary, she renewed her loving consent to the Father's will. As the mourning of the widow called forth the miracle at Naim, our Lady's sorrow calls forth God's mercy on her adopted children, and resurrection for souls dead in sin.

vv. 18–23

Did St John the Baptist's faith in Christ grow uncertain, as he languished in the prison of Herod, tetrarch of Galilee? No. St John had been sanctified in his mother's womb. While still an unborn child, he had *leapt for joy* when Jesus drew near. When, as a man, he finally looked upon Him, the Holy Spirit inspired the Baptist to speak words which the Church repeats each day: *Behold, the Lamb of God*. When he baptised Him, it was granted to St John to see the heavens opened and the Spirit descend in the form of a dove. Until the very end of his short life, he remained *a burning and shining lamp*.

Why then does St John, from his prison cell, send two of his disciples to ask the Lord: *Art thou he that is to come, or look we for another?* Not for his benefit, but for theirs. There was some tension between the disciples of the Baptist and those of our Lord; at least, John's disciples were not sure what to think

24 And when the messengers of John were departed, he began to speak to the multitudes concerning John. What went ye out into the desert to see? a reed shaken with the wind?

25 But what went you out to see? a man clothed in soft garments? Behold they that are in costly apparel and live delicately, are in the houses of kings.

26 But what went you out to see? a prophet? Yea, I say to you, and more than a prophet.

27 This is he of whom it is written: Behold I send my angel before thy face, who shall prepare thy way before thee.

28 For I say to you: Amongst those that are born of women, there is not a greater prophet that John the Baptist. But he that is the lesser in the kingdom of God, is greater than he.

of this Rabbi who had just come from Nazareth and who was already proving more popular than their own teacher.[1] True, the Baptist, in the presence of his own disciples, had borne explicit witness to Christ; but now, knowing perhaps that he will soon die, he wants their faith to be strengthened by spending time in the presence of the Lord Himself.

Christ, understanding His cousin's intention, allows the two messengers to perceive what theology calls the 'signs of credibility'. These are outward events, which people can recognise by their natural powers, but which bear witness to some supernatural truth. The two most striking such signs are miracles and the fulfilment of prophecies.

Christ therefore works miracles for the two disciples, and mentions two prophecies from Isaias. Isaias had foretold that when God came to save His people, *the lame* would *walk*, *the blind* would *see* and the deaf would hear. Our Lord works these miracles, and even adds others which the prophet had not mentioned, perhaps to show that God always does more than we had hoped. He also mentions Isaias's prophecy that the *poor*, or humble, would be evangelised, something which John's disciples now see happening. Thus, both of the signs of credibility — miracles and prophecies — are set before them.

vv. 24–28

As the two disciples return to their master, our Lord begins to speak to the crowd about his cousin, doing two things. First, He praises him. He does not praise him while the two disciples are still present, so as to avoid even the appearance of flattery. But once they have gone, in case anyone in the crowd supposes that it is John himself who needed to be reassured, our Lord lets them see the firmness of John's faith, using a 'contrary similitude'. Of all men in the world, and though he was often to be seen on the side of a river, John was least like a *reed, shaken with the wind*; that is, John did not change his beliefs in accord with public opinion. And lest anyone should imagine that the Baptist's imprisonment by Herod had worn away his constancy,

---

1 See Jn. 3:26.

Christ draws their attention to his cousin's detachment from the pleasures of the senses. The crowd must have smiled when He asked them whether they had gone *out into the desert to see a man dressed in soft robes*, given that John wore a rough garment of camel's hair. *They that are in soft garments are in the houses of kings*; and not, by implication, in their prisons.

Secondly, and as a result, our Lord seems to continue the theme of the signs of credibility. Elsewhere, in a conversation with some of the Jewish authorities in Jerusalem, He reminds them of the testimony which He had received from St John when the Baptist was still at liberty. *You sent to John*, Christ told the Jews on that occasion, *and he gave testimony to the truth. Not that I receive testimony from man: but I say these things, that you may be saved.* It is therefore important for the preaching of the gospel, and the salvation of souls, that the honour of John the Baptist be vindicated. If John appeared to be uncertain about our Lord's mission, that would cause others, also, to hesitate. This is another reason why, without humiliating the two messengers by making it obvious that *they* are the ones who need their faith strengthened, Christ nevertheless allows the crowd to see that John is not the man to waver in his confession of faith under the stress of persecution.

But why does He say to the messengers: *Blessed is he that shall not be scandalized in me?* Why would anyone be scandalized by one who works miracles, or preaches to the lowly? It is not the miracles that will be an occasion of scandal, except for those people who are worst disposed, and who will accuse Him of doing them by an evil spirit. Our Lord is surely looking ahead to the time when, by His Father's will, He will cease to perform miracles, and enter instead into His Passion. For although Isaias had also prophesied that the Saviour would come as a suffering Servant to offer His life for the sins of the people, this part of his prophetic oracles, alien as it is to the aspirations of human nature, was neglected or misunderstood by our Lord's contemporaries. When therefore men saw Him crucified, and apparently unable to respond to the taunt of the chief priests, their faith would be severely tried. Where now were the signs

29 And all the people hearing, and the publicans, justified God, being baptized with John's baptism.

30 But the Pharisees and the lawyers despised the counsel of God against themselves, being not baptized by him.

31 And the Lord said: Whereunto then shall I liken the men of this generation? and to what are they like?

32 They are like to children sitting in the marketplace, and speaking one to another, and saying: We have piped to you, and you have not danced: we have mourned, and you have not wept.

33 For John the Baptist came neither eating bread nor drinking wine; and you say: He hath a devil.

34 The Son of man is come eating and drinking: and you say: Behold a man that is a glutton and a drinker of wine, a friend of publicans and sinners.

35 And wisdom is justified by all her children.

36 And one of the Pharisees desired him to eat with him. And he went into the house of the Pharisee, and sat down to meat.

37 And behold a woman that was in the city, a sinner, when she knew that he sat at meat in the Pharisee's house, brought an alabaster box of ointment;

38 And standing behind at his feet, she began to wash his feet, with tears, and wiped them with the hairs of her head, and kissed his feet, and anointed them with the ointment.

of credibility? They were still there, since the prophecies of the passion were being fulfilled.

If John is *more than a prophet*, since he did not simply recognise the Son of God from afar and in a vision, why is *the lesser*, or the least, *in the kingdom of heaven greater than he*? John is still a wayfarer, living by faith and hope and subject to bodily necessities; those who attain the kingdom, even though their degree of sanctity may be *lesser* than his, are *greater* in this respect. By these words, Christ encourages those who are discouraged that so great a prophet could be so maltreated.

vv. 29–35

The people *justified God*; that is, Christ's praise of the Baptist strengthens them in their conviction of John's holiness, and thus prompts them to praise God whose holiness is revealed by John's mission. The *Pharisees and lawyers* — the latter as it were the theologians of the old covenant — *despised the counsel of God*, that is, they despised John for his poverty. Our Lord points out their inconsistency; they belittle John because he led an extraordinary life, and Himself because, during His public ministry, He led a common and accessible one. They have no more grasp of divine *wisdom* than would *children in the marketplace*, amusing themselves now with one game, now with another. But beneath this inconsistency lies the sinister consistency of unbelief.

vv. 36–50

St Gregory the Great's belief that the woman in the house of *Simon the Pharisee* was St Mary Magdalen, as well as being embedded in western liturgical tradition and supported by private revelations, also fits well with the record of the gospel. From St John we learn that Mary, the sister of Martha, had *anointed the Lord with ointment and wiped his feet with her hair*, and that she repeats the act on the eve of Palm Sunday. On this latter occasion, Christ says that she is to *keep* the ointment that remains *against the day of my burial*, and St Mary Magdalen accordingly

39 And the Pharisee, who had invited him, seeing it, spoke within himself, saying: This man, if he were a prophet, would know surely who and what manner of woman this is that toucheth him, that she is a sinner.

40 And Jesus answering, said to him: Simon, I have somewhat to say to thee. But he said: Master, say it.

41 A certain creditor had two debtors, the one who owed five hundred pence, and the other fifty.

42 And whereas they had not wherewith to pay, he forgave them both. Which therefore of the two loveth him most?

43 Simon answering, said: I suppose that he to whom he forgave most. And he said to him: Thou hast judged rightly.

44 And turning to the woman, he said unto Simon: Dost thou see this woman? I entered into thy house, thou gavest me no water for my feet; but she with tears hath washed my feet, and with her hairs hath wiped them.

45 Thou gavest me no kiss; but she, since she came in, hath not ceased to kiss my feet.

46 My head with oil thou didst not anoint; but she with ointment hath anointed my feet.

47 Wherefore I say to thee: Many sins are forgiven her, because she hath loved much. But to whom less is forgiven, he loveth less.

48 And he said to her: Thy sins are forgiven thee.

49 And they that sat at meat with him began to say within themselves: Who is this that forgiveth sins also?

50 And he said to the woman: Thy faith hath made thee safe, go in peace.

---

men, the degree to which debts are forgiven tends to give rise to a proportionate love, between God and the soul this order is reversed: love itself has the power to destroy debt. Since Simon had judged rashly both of Christ and of Magdalen, it is fitting that this truth about the inward relations of the Creator and the creature be concealed from him for the present.

This episode is therefore also a sign of Christ's divinity. Magdalen's sins are forgiven by her love for Christ; but it is only by loving *God* that sins are forgiven.

comes to anoint the Body on Easter morning. St Luke himself suggests this identification by mentioning Magdalen for the first time immediately after the scene in the Pharisee's house, while simple tact would explain why she was not named during the scene itself. Again, the sister of Martha is described as sitting at Christ's feet in chapter ten, and falling down at His feet in St John, chapter eleven, while St Mary Magdalen is described, by implication, as holding Christ's feet in St John, chapter twenty. All this tends almost irresistibly to build up a portrait of one woman, a portrait that corresponds to the woman in this scene.

When the Lord says: *Many sins are forgiven her, because she hath loved much*, is her love a cause or a sign? That is, does He mean: "Her love for me has blotted out her sins", or: "From her love you can see that her sins must have previously been forgiven"? The parable of the two creditors would seem to indicate the latter explanation, and yet the episode is often used to illustrate the role of charity in *effecting* the justification of the sinner.[2] An objection to seeing her love as simply a sign of justification is that a man cannot perceive that his sins have been forgiven, as a human debtor can know when his human creditor has released him, and consequently begin to love him. Another objection is that it does not always happen, in fact, that the charity of sinners is in proportion to the gravity of the sins which they are severally forgiven. It seems therefore that we should follow the traditional interpretation, of Mary's love as a *cause* of her forgiveness.

Why then the parable? Simon's ambiguous attitude toward Christ, inviting Him to dine and calling Him *Master*, yet also treating Him with reserve and suspicion, makes it fitting that the Lord tell him a parable that will partly express and partly veil the truth. The truth which it expresses, and which Simon grasps, is that as among men, so also between God and the soul there is a proportion between the force of love and the forgiveness of debts. The truth that remains veiled is that whereas among

---

2   For example, the collect for her feast: "Grant to us, most clement Father, that as blessed Mary Magdalen, by loving our Lord Jesus Christ above all things obtained the pardon of her sins, so she may win perpetual blessedness for us by her prayers before Thy mercy" (Dominican missal).

1 And it came to pass afterwards, that he travelled through the cities and towns, preaching and evangelizing the kingdom of God; and the twelve with him:

2 And certain women who had been healed of evil spirits and infirmities; Mary who is called Magdalen, out of whom seven devils were gone forth,

3 And Joanna the wife of Chusa, Herod's steward, and Susanna, and many others who ministered unto him of their substance.

4 And when a very great multitude was gathered together, and hastened out of the cities unto him, he spoke by a similitude.

5 The sower went out to sow his seed. And as he sowed, some fell by the wayside, and it was trodden down, and the fowls of the air devoured it.

6 And other some fell upon a rock: and as soon as it was sprung up, it withered away, because it had no moisture.

7 And other some fell among thorns, and the thorns growing up with it, choked it.

8 And other some fell upon good ground; and being sprung up, yielded fruit a hundredfold. Saying these things, he cried out: He that hath ears to hear, let him hear.

9 And his disciples asked him what this parable might be.

10 To whom he said: To you it is given to know the mystery of the kingdom of God; but to the rest in parables, that seeing they may not see, and hearing may not understand.

11 Now the parable is this: The seed is the word of God.

12 And they by the wayside are they that hear; then the devil cometh, and taketh the word out of their heart, lest believing they should be saved.

13 Now they upon the rock, are they who when they hear, receive the word with joy: and these have no roots; for they believe for a while, and in time of temptation, they fall away.

14 And that which fell among thorns, are they who have

vv. 1–18

I T IS WHEN HE HAD BEGUN TO ATTRACT *A very great multitude* that our Lord tells the parable of the Sower. He is giving the apostles to understand that later on, when they find themselves preaching to great numbers, they mustn't suppose that their work is done or that all their hearers will reach salvation. We learn from this parable that *the devil* interests himself in preaching, more indeed than many of those to whom it is directed. Hence even St Paul asked for prayers for himself, that he might announce the word of God clearly.

The *roots* which the second group lack are the virtues. As the roots of a plant are necessary to it yet grow imperceptibly, so the virtues grow by repetition of good acts.

Cares seem very different from *riches* and bodily *pleasures,* yet all are compared to thorns. Why is this? All three tend to wound the minds of fallen men, in the absence of the virtues.

The Lord encourages the desire of His disciples to understand the parables. They are to be the candle enlightening those *who come in* to the Church. He does not wish this light to be covered *with a vessel* of riches and consequent worldly cares, nor put *under a bed* of pleasure. The disciple must *take heed* how he receives Christ's words: *for whosoever hath* diligence in reflecting on them, *to him shall be* given insight in understanding and fruit in preaching and other good works*; and whoever hath not* this diligence, *that* right to be called a disciple *which he thinketh he hath, shall be taken away from him* publicly on the last day, when *hidden* things *are known and come abroad.*

For *the rest* of mankind, His words remain *parables, that seeing they may not see*: in justice, as a punishment for culpable incuriosity; and in mercy, both lest they increase their punishment by rejecting that which they would then have more clearly understood, but also so that some at least may desire and eventually attain *the mystery.*

heard, and going their way, are choked with the cares and riches and pleasures of this life, and yield no fruit.

15 But that on the good ground, are they who in a good and perfect heart, hearing the word, keep it, and bring forth fruit in patience.

16 Now no man lighting a candle covereth it with a vessel, or putteth it under a bed; but setteth it upon a candlestick, that they who come in may see the light.

17 For there is not anything secret that shall not be made manifest, nor hidden, that shall not be known and come abroad.

18 Take heed therefore how you hear. For whosoever hath, to him shall be given: and whosoever hath not, that also which he thinketh he hath, shall be taken away from him.

19 And his mother and brethren came unto him; and they could not come at him for the crowd.

20 And it was told him: Thy mother and thy brethren stand without, desiring to see thee.

21 Who answering, said to them: My mother and my brethren are they who hear the word of God, and do it.

22 And it came to pass on a certain day that he went into a little ship with his disciples, and he said to them: Let us go over to the other side of the lake. And they launched forth.

23 And when they were sailing, he slept; and there came down a storm of wind upon the lake, and they were filled, and were in danger.

24 And they came and awaked him, saying: Master, we perish. But he, arising, rebuked the wind and the rage of the water; and it ceased, and there was a calm.

25 And he said to them: Where is your faith? Who being afraid, wondered, saying one to another: Who is this, (think you), that he commandeth both the winds and the sea, and they obey him?

26 And they sailed to the country of the Gerasens, which is over against Galilee.

vv. 19–21

Like St Joseph, the Lord did not wish that the Blessed Virgin Mary should be put on display before a multitude who would be unable to appreciate her. He knew also that in her humility she did not wish to receive the honour that men would naturally bestow on the mother of a great preacher and thaumaturge. Hence, when He receives the message that she is present with His brethren, He turns the attention of the crowd away from them.

vv. 22–39

Since there is a *legion* of unclean spirits possessing a man on the other side of the lake, it would not be surprising if the storm were an attempt by the devil to keep away this mysterious Exorcist. That would explain why Christ did not simply command but *rebuked* the wind and sea; rebuking in effect the fallen angels using them as instruments.

Why do the devils not wish *to go into the abyss*, that is, to hell? They fear being punished there by their masters, and being mocked, for their failure on earth. They seem to realise that the only alternative that God intends to offer is that they be sent into the swine. Christ allows this as proof of the reality of the exorcism and to symbolise for us the nature of unclean spirits by means of these unclean animals.

27 And when he was come forth to the land, there met him a certain man who had a devil now a very long time, and he wore no clothes, neither did he abide in a house, but in the sepulchres.

28 And when he saw Jesus, he fell down before him; and crying out with a loud voice, he said: What have I to do with thee, Jesus, Son of the most high God? I beseech thee, do not torment me.

29 For he commanded the unclean spirit to go out of the man. For many times it seized him, and he was bound with chains, and kept in fetters; and breaking the bonds, he was driven by the devil into the deserts.

30 And Jesus asked him, saying: What is thy name? But he said: Legion; because many devils were entered into him.

31 And they besought him that he would not command them to go into the abyss.

32 And there was there a herd of many swine feeding on the mountain; and they besought him that he would suffer them to enter into them. And he suffered them.

33 The devils therefore went out of the man and entered into the swine; and the herd ran violently down a steep place into the lake, and were stifled.

34 Which when they that fed them saw done, they fled away, and told it in the city and in the villages.

35 And they went out to see what was done; and they came to Jesus, and found the man, out of whom the devils were departed, sitting at his feet, clothed, and in his right mind; and they were afraid.

36 And they also that had seen, told them how he had been healed from the legion.

37 And all the multitude of the country of the Gerasens besought him to depart from them; for they were taken with great fear. And he, going up into the ship, returned back again.

38 Now the man, out of whom the devils were departed, besought him that he might be with him. But Jesus sent him away, saying:

39 Return to thy house and tell how great things God hath done to thee. And he went through the whole city, publishing how great things Jesus had done to him.

The exorcised man is not allowed to accompany Christ and the apostles on their preaching tours, perhaps because he is a gentile, but instead told to bear witness in his home-town. He thus becomes the first of those who evangelise not as ministers of the Church but by giving testimony of their own conversion.

40 And it came to pass, that when Jesus was returned, the multitude received him: for they were all waiting for him.

41 And behold there came a man whose name was Jairus, and he was a ruler of the synagogue: and he fell down at the feet of Jesus, beseeching him that he would come into his house:

42 For he had an only daughter, almost twelve years old, and she was dying. And it happened as he went, that he was thronged by the multitudes.

43 And there was a certain woman having an issue of blood twelve years, who had bestowed all her substance on physicians, and could not be healed by any.

44 She came behind him and touched the hem of his garment; and immediately the issue of her blood stopped.

45 And Jesus said: Who is it that touched me? And all denying, Peter and they that were with him said: Master, the multitudes throng and press thee, and dost thou say, Who touched me?

46 And Jesus said: Somebody hath touched me; for I know that virtue is gone out from me.

47 And the woman seeing that she was not hid, came trembling, and fell down before his feet, and declared before all the people for what cause she had touched him, and how she was immediately healed.

48 But he said to her: Daughter, thy faith hath made thee whole; go thy way in peace.

49 As he was yet speaking, there cometh one to the ruler of the synagogue, saying to him: Thy daughter is dead, trouble him not.

50 And Jesus hearing this word, answered the father of the maid: Fear not; believe only, and she shall be safe.

51 And when he was come to the house, he suffered not any man to go in with him, but Peter and James and John, and the father and mother of the maiden.

52 And all wept and mourned for her. But he said: Weep not; the maid is not dead, but sleepeth.

53 And they laughed him to scorn, knowing that she was dead.

54 But he taking her by the hand, cried out, saying: Maid, arise.

vv. 40–56

The faith of the woman with the haemorrhage is rewarded with a miracle that manifests our Lord's divinity in a strange and wonderful way. He cures her, as far as we can judge from the gospel, in a unique manner: without the normal human activity of intellect and will. Hence, He can ask: *Who touched me?* It is as if to say: "I did not come to know this person by sight or hearing and then because of this knowledge choose to heal her". This miracle proves a doctrine which it would cost the Church much trouble to vindicate against powerful heretics in the seventh century, namely, the doctrine of the two wills of Jesus Christ, one human and one divine.

The woman herself, who had been afraid to go to meet Christ in person, or to speak to Him face-to-face, was not afraid to display her gratitude. It is said that she lived in the town of Caesarea Philippi, and had a statue made there which displayed her kneeling at His feet, and Jesus stretching His hand over her in blessing. The distinguished historian Eusebius, who was born around the year 270 and who was a bishop in Palestine, tells us that he had seen the statue, and that according to the tradition of the townsfolk, it was indeed this woman who had had it made.[1]

This miracle is embedded within another one, the raising of Jairus's daughter. The Fathers of the Church see a mystery in this. Christ came into the world to be *the servant of the circumcision,* that is, of the Jews. He even told the disciples, before His passion: *Go not in the way of the pagans, nor to any city of the Samaritans.* He came, that is, to raise up the daughter of Israel, or those who belonged to the synagogue. Yet Christ's work of healing the Jews was, to speak in a human fashion, interrupted. The chief priests blocked it, crying out: *We have no king but Caesar.* So, the Jews as a whole remaining unconverted, the Gentiles met our Lord and were healed. They did not see His Face, since He had already ascended, just as the woman with the haemorrhage did not see His Face when she was healed. It was enough for

1 *Ecclesiastical History,* book 7, chapter 18.

55 And her spirit returned, and she arose immediately. And he bid them give her to eat.

56 And her parents were astonished, whom he charged to tell no man what was done.

them to touch *the hem of his garment*, that is, the preaching and sacraments of His Church.

Even the years match. The woman had been suffering from *an issue of blood twelve years*. But Jairus's daughter *was almost twelve years old*. She had been born, therefore, just after this woman started to lose her strength. This corresponds to the mystery of the Jews and the Gentiles: St Augustine tells us that God called Abraham, the father of the Jewish people, just after the Gentiles had begun to worship idols, by which, over the centuries, they became continuously weaker, despite all the efforts of their learned men — their *physicians* — to put them right.

But once the woman has been healed, our Saviour resumes His journey. He arrives at last at the synagogue, and though they laugh Him to scorn for saying that the dead one is but sleeping, He puts them outside, and brings the dead girl to life. So it will be, no doubt, toward the end of the world. The Lord will speak to the Jewish people, and they will hear and awake; and thus *All Israel will be saved*.

1 Then calling together the twelve apostles, he gave them power and authority over all devils, and to cure diseases.

2 And he sent them to preach the kingdom of God, and to heal the sick.

3 And he said to them: Take nothing for your journey; neither staff, nor scrip, nor bread, nor money; neither have two coats.

4 And whatsoever house you shall enter into, abide there, and depart not from thence.

5 And whosoever will not receive you, when ye go out of that city, shake off even the dust of your feet, for a testimony against them.

6 And going out, they went about through the towns, preaching the gospel, and healing everywhere.

7 Now Herod, the tetrarch, heard of all things that were done by him; and he was in a doubt, because it was said

8 By some, that John was risen from the dead: but by other some, that Elias had appeared; and by others, that one of the old prophets was risen again.

9 And Herod said: John I have beheaded; but who is this of whom I hear such things? And he sought to see him.

10 And the apostles, when they were returned, told him all they had done. And taking them, he went aside into a desert place, apart, which belongeth to Bethsaida.

11 Which when the people knew, they followed him; and he received them, and spoke to them of the kingdom of God, and healed them who had need of healing.

12 Now the day began to decline. And the twelve came and said to him: Send away the multitude, that going into the towns and villages round about, they may lodge and get victuals; for we are here in a desert place.

13 But he said to them: Give you them to eat. And they said: We have no more than five loaves and two fishes; unless perhaps we should go and buy food for all this multitude.

vv. 1–9

THE TWELVE ARE SENT OUT IN ENTIRE dependence on providence. Our Lord wished the divine protection of their mission to be thus made manifest. Later, in chapter twenty-two, we shall see Him send them out in a different way.

In St John's gospel, at the washing of the feet, *the dust of the feet* will symbolise those small faults from which preachers cannot be immune, especially when in contact with the world at large. The disciples must *shake off* this dust when people do not receive them, since fruitless preaching obliges the preachers themselves to further conversion.

The people suggest that *John* or *one of the old prophets was risen again*, but that *Elias had appeared*, since it is believed that Elias has not died but is preserved by divine power in some hidden part of creation.

vv. 10–17

From St Mark's gospel, we learn that all the numbers in the two multiplications of the loaves and fishes have a hidden meaning. We may see this first multiplication as representing Christ's sacrifice of Himself upon the Cross, by which He founds the Church. The bread and fish represent Himself: *five*, the number of the loaves, is the number of the living body, with its five senses, while the *two fish*, since fish live hidden from man, may be taken to represent His soul and His divinity. All this He offers to the Father, as on the Cross. The bread is torn apart but remains at the end, because by the offering of His body on the Cross, He brought His mystical body into being; and this mystical body is symbolised by *twelve*, the number of the apostles, on whom the Church is built. *Five thousand men are*

14 Now there were about five thousand men. And he said to his disciples: Make them sit down by fifties in a company.

15 And they did so; and made them all sit down.

16 And taking the five loaves and the two fishes, he looked up to heaven, and blessed them; and he broke, and distributed to his disciples, to set before the multitude.

17 And they did all eat and were filled. And there were taken up of fragments that remained to them, twelve baskets.

18 And it came to pass, as he was alone praying, his disciples also were with him: and he asked them, saying: Whom do the people say that I am?

19 But they answered and said: John the Baptist; but some say Elias; and others say that one of the former prophets is risen again.

20 And he said to them: But whom do you say that I am? Simon Peter answering, said: The Christ of God.

21 But he strictly charging them, commanded they should tell this to no man.

22 Saying: The Son of man must suffer many things and be rejected by the ancients and chief priests and scribes, and be killed, and the third day rise again.

23 And he said to all: If any man will come after me, let him deny himself, and take up his cross daily, and follow me.

24 For whosoever will save his life, shall lose it; for he that shall lose his life for my sake, shall save it.

25 For what is a man advantaged, if he gain the whole world, and lose himself, and cast away himself?

26 For he that shall be ashamed of me and of my words, of him the Son of man shall be ashamed, when he shall come in his majesty, and that of his Father, and of the holy angels.

27 But I tell you of a truth: There are some standing here that shall not taste death, till they see the kingdom of God.

fed because Christ's sacrifice on the Cross, though a mystery, can be grasped even by those who live according to the senses. The second multiplication, which St Luke does not narrate, will refer then to Christ's sacrifice of Himself in the Church, through the holy Mass.

vv. 18–27

Even though *his disciples were with him, he was alone praying.* "None can be a sharer of the inward things of Christ", wrote St Ambrose.

St Luke omits the promise to St Peter of the keys of the Kingdom, perhaps to conceal from the pagans to whom his gospel may come the identity of the earthly head of the Christians.

Why does our Lord *strictly* charge the disciples *to tell no man* of His messiahship? Such preaching, coupled with the miracles, would have confirmed the Jews in their erroneous hope for a temporal Messias. Hence the apostles do not preach Him as *the Christ of God* until after His death and resurrection. But although He curbs the public use of the word itself, He allows St John the Baptist to describe Him as *he that baptizeth with the Holy Ghost* and as the one who was *to be made manifest in Israel.*

He says *to all* that they must aim either at temporal or at eternal success, seeking glory either from *the ancients and the chief priests and the scribes,* or else from *the Son of man* and *his Father* and *the holy angels.* The one who does not look steadily toward eternity may either *lose himself* entirely, in hell, or else he may simply 'suffer loss', as we may also translate the phrase rendered as *cast himself away.* The same word is used by St Paul in chapter three of the first epistle to the Corinthians, speaking of the loss suffered by a Christian who, though just, commits venial sins that must be burnt away. Hence, we may see in this verse of the gospel a reference to purgatory.

28 And it came to pass about eight days after these words, that he took Peter, and James, and John, and went up into a mountain to pray.

29 And whilst he prayed, the shape of his countenance was altered, and his raiment became white and glittering.

30 And behold two men were talking with him. And they were Moses and Elias,

31 Appearing in majesty. And they spoke of his decease that he should accomplish in Jerusalem.

32 But Peter and they that were with him were heavy with sleep. And waking, they saw his glory, and the two men that stood with him.

33 And it came to pass, that as they were departing from him, Peter saith to Jesus: Master, it is good for us to be here; and let us make three tabernacles, one for thee, and one for Moses, and one for Elias; not knowing what he said.

34 And as he spoke these things, there came a cloud, and overshadowed them; and they were afraid, when they entered into the cloud.

35 And a voice came out of the cloud, saying: This is my beloved Son; hear him.

36 And whilst the voice was uttered, Jesus was found alone. And they held their peace and told no man in those days any of these things which they had seen.

Lest His words seem too hard and depress His hearers, He encourages them by telling them how close the Kingdom of God is. It will appear in His transfiguration.

vv. 28–36

Why does the Lord not take all the apostles to the *mountain, to pray*? Perhaps if all had seen Moses and Elias, it would have been impossible for the matter to have remained private, and He did not choose that so great a mystery become common talk. Again, He wished that though all were brothers and apostles, there should even among them be a hierarchy, lest anyone later suppose that the sacrament of baptism means that none of the faithful have authority in regard to others.

Christ's transfiguration was the natural result of the beatific vision that He possessed in His human soul from the beginning. It was only by a special divine dispensation, or 'economy', that His body was not always glorious. The glory is allowed to appear now to reassure the apostles before His passion. Perhaps also it is for our Lord Himself the first-fruits of His reward: hence, just before the Passion, the Father's voice will be heard, saying: *I have glorified, and I shall glorify.*

Moses and Elias speak with Him *of his decease*, or 'exodus', *that he should accomplish*, since both men foreshadowed it in their own day: Moses, by passing through the Red Sea, and Elias by being taken miraculously from the earth. Again, Elias comes because he is still alive though in an unknown place, while Moses's soul is brought from the Limbo of the Fathers and re-united to his body, to manifest Jesus as *Lord of the dead and of the living*, as St Paul will say.

One might have expected the three apostles to be afraid when they saw *Moses and Elias appearing in majesty*, rather than when they entered the cloud, since there is nothing strange about a cloud on a mountain-top. But this cloud, as we learn from St Matthew, was a bright one, and a sign of the presence of the Holy Ghost.

37 And it came to pass the day following, when they came down from the mountain, there met him a great multitude.

38 And behold a man among the crowd cried out, saying: Master, I beseech thee, look upon my son, because he is my only one.

39 And lo, a spirit seizeth him, and he suddenly crieth out, and he throweth him down and teareth him, so that he foameth; and bruising him, he hardly departeth from him.

40 And I desired thy disciples to cast him out, and they could not.

41 And Jesus answering, said: O faithless and perverse generation, how long shall I be with you, and suffer you? Bring hither thy son.

42 And as he was coming to him, the devil threw him down, and tore him.

43 And Jesus rebuked the unclean spirit, and cured the boy, and restored him to his father.

44 And all were astonished at the mighty power of God. But while all wondered at all the things he did, he said to his disciples: Lay you up in your hearts these words, for it shall come to pass, that the Son of man shall be delivered into the hands of men.

45 But they understood not this word; and it was hid from them, so that they perceived it not. And they were afraid to ask him concerning this word.

46 And there entered a thought into them, which of them should be greater.

47 But Jesus seeing the thoughts of their heart, took a child and set him by him,

48 And said to them: Whosoever shall receive this child in my name, receiveth me; and whosoever shall receive me, receiveth him that sent me. For he that is the lesser among you all, he is the greater.

vv. 37–43

The eternal Father shows the three disciples His only, *beloved Son* at the top of the mountain; at its foot, a human father presents the other disciples with his *only one*, a possessed lunatic. Is it the poignancy of the contrast that leads our Lord to reveal the thought of His heart, not by an outburst of impatience, but by a noble and loving protest against the faithlessness of His contemporaries: *How long shall I be with you and suffer you?*

Why can the disciples not exorcise the boy, when at the start of the chapter, the twelve receive *power over all devils*? Either the nine were absent; or else this power, though conferred, could not be fully wielded by those who had not sufficiently prayed and fasted, as we may gather from St Matthew and St Mark.

vv. 43–48

One can see why the disciples might have found it hard to believe that their Master would be overpowered by men, given His miracles, but why was it hard for them even to understand His meaning? Perhaps they thought that He could *be delivered into the hands of men* only by some angelic intervention. They did not yet grasp that He would deliver Himself up. It was perhaps in thinking confusedly of the future time when He would no longer be with them, that they began to wonder *which of them should* then *be greater.* Yet did they not already know that it was to be Peter, to whom the keys of the kingdom had been promised? They may have wondered whether he had forfeited the promise, because of the words: *Get behind me, Satan.*

Rather than repeat His teaching about Peter's primacy, as He will do at the Last Supper, Christ gives them a more rudimentary lesson, necessary for understanding this primacy. The hierarchy in His earthly Church exists to glorify the Father, and hence to glorify the Son, and so to serve, or *receive,* those who are members of the Son; but such service is greater, insofar as it derives no profit from the earthly excellence of those who

49 And John, answering, said: Master, we saw a certain man casting out devils in thy name, and we forbade him, because he followeth not with us.

50 And Jesus said to him: Forbid him not; for he that is not against you, is for you.

51 And it came to pass, when the days of his assumption were accomplishing, that he steadfastly set his face to go to Jerusalem.

52 And he sent messengers before his face; and going, they entered into a city of the Samaritans, to prepare for him.

53 And they received him not, because his face was of one going to Jerusalem.

54 And when his disciples James and John had seen this, they said: Lord, wilt thou that we command fire to come down from heaven, and consume them?

55 And turning, he rebuked them, saying: You know not of what spirit you are.

56 The Son of man came not to destroy souls, but to save. And they went into another town.

57 And it came to pass, as they walked in the way, that a certain man said to him: I will follow thee withersoever thou goest.

58 Jesus said to him: The foxes have holes, and the birds of the air nests; but the Son of man hath not where to lay his head.

59 But he said to another: Follow me. And he said: Lord, suffer me first to go, and to bury my father.

60 And Jesus said to him: Let the dead bury their dead: but go thou and preach the kingdom of God.

are served, as is most apparent when it is rendered to a *child*; therefore, Christian greatness consists in humility.

vv. 49–50

St John's question continues the subject of authority. Christ does not deny that the apostles had the authority to *forbid* the man from exorcising, but, as we learn from St Mark's account, He bids them tolerate this irregular activity because one may prudently judge that for now at least, it will have good consequences. Similarly, the Church often allows baptised non-Catholics to exercise such sacramental powers as they possess, for example allowing validly ordained non-Catholic priests to hear confessions.

vv. 51–56

St James and St John must have had in mind how the prophet Elias, whom they had so recently seen, had twice brought down *fire from heaven* upon the soldiers whom the idolatrous king of Israel sent to arrest him. Elias was moved by divine inspiration thus to manifest God's judgement on idolatry. Since Christ was not to judge the world until the last day, His two apostles were not moved on this occasion by divine inspiration, but rather by some other *spirit*, such as a natural, unregulated zeal for His honour.

vv. 57–62

In becoming the *Son of man* who *hath not where to lay his head*, the Word also illustrated a general truth. Although God could have willed things otherwise, yet as it is, the sons of men, alone among visible creatures, cannot satisfy their desires on earth or by exercising their natural powers, but only after death and by grace.

We need not suppose that the second man's *father* was already *dead*: it is likely enough to be an idiom meaning 'let me wait until

61 And another said: I will follow thee, Lord; but let me first take my leave of them that are at my house.

62 Jesus said to him: No man putting his hand to the plough, and looking back, is fit for the kingdom of God.

he has died'. Our Lord's answer implies that those who desire to enter the religious life should not be deterred for fear that there will not be enough people left to do the necessary work of the world. St Thomas Aquinas remarks that such a fear is foolish, like imagining that a river will run dry if I drink from it.

Christ seems to wish to give greater force to these teachings about discipleship, by delivering them after He has bidden farewell to Nazareth, which He must have dearly loved, for the last time.

1 And after these things the Lord appointed also other seventy-two: and he sent them two and two before his face into every city and place whither he himself was to come.

2 And he said to them: The harvest indeed is great, but the labourers are few. Pray ye therefore the Lord of the harvest, that he send labourers into his harvest.

3 Go: Behold I send you as lambs among wolves.

4 Carry neither purse, nor scrip, nor shoes; and salute no man by the way.

5 Into whatsoever house you enter, first say: Peace be to this house.

6 And if the son of peace be there, your peace shall rest upon him; but if not, it shall return to you.

7 And in the same house, remain, eating and drinking such things as they have: for the labourer is worthy of his hire. Remove not from house to house.

8 And into what city soever you enter, and they receive you, eat such things as are set before you.

9 And heal the sick that are therein and say to them: The kingdom of God is come nigh unto you.

10 But into whatsoever city you enter, and they receive you not, going forth into the streets thereof, say:

11 Even the very dust of your city that cleaveth to us, we wipe off against you. Yet know this, that the kingdom of God is at hand.

12 I say to you, it shall be more tolerable at that day for Sodom, than for that city.

13 Woe to thee, Corozain, woe to thee, Bethsaida. For if in Tyre and Sidon had been wrought the mighty works that have been wrought in you, they would have done penance long ago, sitting in sackcloth and ashes.

14 But it shall be more tolerable for Tyre and Sidon at the judgement, than for you.

15 And thou, Capharnaum, which art exalted unto heaven, thou shalt be thrust down to hell.

16 He that heareth you, heareth me; and he that despiseth you, despiseth me; and he that despiseth me, despiseth him that sent me.

vv. 1–16

AS THE MESSIAS OF ISRAEL, JESUS SENDS out the seventy-two disciples to call the people to prepare for the Redemption. Enough miracles have been worked, that if *they receive* the disciples *not*, they will now be gravely culpable. He would have them *salute no man by the way*, to show that the hour of decision is sounding, and admits of no delay.

St Luke is the only evangelist to mention this sending out of the seventy-two (or seventy, according to some manuscripts). This could be explained by the fact that he was one of them, as St Epiphanius states. This second mission seems to represent the future mission of the Church to *every city and place whither* Christ *himself was to come* by the solicitations of His grace, that is, to all the peoples of the world. Thus St Augustine observes that the circuit of the world, represented by the twenty-four hours of the day, is to be enlightened by the mystery of the Trinity; hence the number seventy-two.

The disciples, having entered a given town or village, are not to go *from house to house*, lest they seem to be looking for the choicest foods in successive households.

What exactly were they to preach, given that the Lord had commanded them not to say that He was the Messias, and since they did not understand His teaching about His passion? They could at least repeat His moral teaching, and present Him as a prophet whose words must be accepted as the condition for entering the coming kingdom. No doubt they also encouraged and led prayers, before and after their miracles.

In the previous chapter, the twelve were told simply to *shake off the dust from* their *feet for a testimony,* in towns where their mission was rejected, while here the disciples are told to accompany this gesture with words, spoken in public: a sign that the sin is greater, as the Redemption offered is closer. It will be *more tolerable* on the *day* of judgement *for Sodom* than

17 And the seventy-two returned with joy, saying: Lord, the devils also are subject to us in thy name.

18 And he said to them: I saw Satan like lightening falling from heaven.

19 Behold, I have given you power to tread upon serpents and scorpions, and upon all the power of the enemy: and nothing shall hurt you.

20 But yet rejoice not in this, that spirits are subject unto you; but rejoice in this, that your names are written in heaven.

21 In that same hour, he rejoiced in the Holy Ghost, and said: I confess to thee, O Father, Lord of heaven and earth, because thou hast hidden these things from the wise and prudent, and hast revealed them to little ones. Yea, Father, for so it hath seemed good in thy sight.

22 All things are delivered to me by my Father; and no one knoweth who the Son is, but the Father; and who the Father is, but the Son, and to whom the Son will reveal him.

23 And turning to his disciples, he said: Blessed are the eyes that see the things which you see.

24 For I say to you, that many prophets and kings have desired to see the things that you see, and have not seen them; and to hear the things that you hear, and have not heard them.

for such a town, since unbelief, committed against God, is worse than sexual sins, committed against human beings.

Will cities as such be punished and rewarded on the last day? Yes, at least in the sense that those who exercised power within them will be punished or rewarded insofar as they sought, or did not seek, to submit their city to the word of God. Thus *Capharnaum,* which had been *exalted unto heaven* when Jesus and Mary made it their dwelling during His public ministry, will be *thrust down to hell* in the persons of its ruling men. This passage also refutes the error of those today who hold that rulers should desire to heed only natural law and not divine revelation in framing their laws, for in that case Sodom would be lower than Capharnaum.

vv. 17–24

What are the *things hidden from* those who were *wise* in knowing the letter of the Old Testament or who seemed *prudent* in governing? That *all things* were *delivered* to Jesus by His Father, and that only the Father *knoweth who the Son is*: in other words, His messiahship and divinity. By revealing *who the Father is*, He reveals also Himself, since the very notion of a father implies that of a son. *Prophets and* righteous *kings*, not only in Israel but among those such as Melchisedek who lived earlier still, *desired to see* the Son in person made visible *and to hear* His words. Why does He not also say 'many priests'? Perhaps because priests were not so exalted in people's minds as kings and prophets.

25 And behold a certain lawyer stood up, tempting him, and saying, Master, what must I do to possess eternal life?

26 But he said to him: What is written in the law? how readest thou?

27 He answering, said: Thou shalt love the Lord thy God with thy whole heart, and with thy whole soul, and with all thy strength, and with all thy mind: and thy neighbour as thyself.

28 And he said to him: Thou hast answered right: this do, and thou shalt live.

29 But he willing to justify himself, said to Jesus: And who is my neighbour?

30 And Jesus answering, said: A certain man went down from Jerusalem to Jericho, and fell among robbers, who also stripped him, and having wounded him went away, leaving him half dead.

31 And it chanced, that a certain priest went down the same way: and seeing him, passed by.

32 In like manner also a Levite, when he was near the place and saw him, passed by.

33 But a certain Samaritan being on his journey, came near him; and seeing him, was moved with compassion.

34 And going up to him, bound up his wounds, pouring in oil and wine: and setting him upon his own beast, brought him to an inn, and took care of him.

35 And the next day he took out two pence, and gave to the host, and said: Take care of him; and whatsoever thou shalt spend over and above, I, at my return, will repay thee.

36 Which of these three, in thy opinion, was neighbour to him that fell among the robbers?

37 But he said: He that shewed mercy to him. And Jesus said to him: Go, and do thou in like manner.

38 Now it came to pass as they went, that he entered into a certain town: and a certain woman named Martha, received him into her house.

39 And she had a sister called Mary, who sitting also at the Lord's feet, heard his word.

40 But Martha was busy about much serving. Who stood

vv. 25–37

Why must the lawyer *justify himself*, since his answer is good? Perhaps because the very fact that he knew the answer to his question raises the suspicion that he asked it in bad faith: to test Christ under the appearance of seeking instruction.

Our Lord in reply sketches the history of salvation. It is Adam who *went down* by his fall, from *Jerusalem*, that is, intimacy with God, to *Jericho*, which means 'the moon' and hence represents instability. The demons *stripped him* of grace and the other gifts of his original state, leaving all the powers of his soul *wounded*. He was *half-dead*, living in his body but no longer in the spirit.

There was a priesthood already before the Law, yet even when the priests were just men like Abel or Noah, they were themselves going *down the same way* as Adam, fallen like him and destined like him for Sheol. Hence, though *seeing* man's plight, they *passed by*, able to bring no cure before they left this world.

The *Levite* came more *near the place*, since the Law of Moses and its rituals represented more eloquently the wounds of man and the divinely-prepared remedy, but he also *passed by*, accomplishing nothing, since these rituals were empty of healing grace.

The Lord compares Himself to a Samaritan, for the charity that He came to teach surpasses the barriers of family and nation. He is *moved with compassion* at the sight of fallen man, and *came near* to him by putting on *the likeness of sinful flesh*. He institutes the grace-giving sacraments of the new Law, as it were *pouring oil and wine* into man's wounds, and bringing him to the *inn* of the Church. After the day of His mortal life is over, He entrusts him *on the next day* to the *host*, bidding St Peter to feed the flock. *The two pennies* of His own merits and satisfactions will be more than enough to pay for the patient's welfare; yet whatever the shepherds expend of themselves, He *will repay* at His *return*.

vv. 38–41

If this story concerns St Martha and St Mary Magdalene, why would St Luke not state this? Perhaps he wishes to leave room for doubt about which Martha is in question, since the episode shows up an imperfection in her.

and said: Lord, hast thou no care that my sister hath left me alone to serve? speak to her therefore, that she help me.

41 And the Lord answering, said to her: Martha, Martha, thou art careful, and art troubled about many things:

42 But one thing is necessary. Mary hath chosen the best part, which shall not be taken away from her.

Mary's part will *not be taken away from her,* since contemplation will remain in heaven, when there will be no more need for works of hospitality.

CHAPTER 11

1 And it came to pass, that as he was in a certain place praying, when he ceased, one of his disciples said to him: Lord, teach us to pray, as John also taught his disciples.

2 And he said to them: When you pray, say: Father, hallowed be thy name. Thy kingdom come.

3 Give us this day our daily bread.

4 And forgive us our sins, for we also forgive every one that is indebted to us. And lead us not into temptation.

5 And he said to them: Which of you shall have a friend, and shall go to him at midnight, and shall say to him: Friend, lend me three loaves,

6 Because a friend of mine is come off his journey to me, and I have not what to set before him.

7 And he from within should answer, and say: Trouble me not, the door is now shut, and my children are with me in bed; I cannot rise and give thee.

8 Yet if he shall continue knocking, I say to you, although he will not rise and give him, because he is his friend; yet, because of his importunity, he will rise, and give him as many as he needeth.

vv. 1–4

EARLIER, CHRIST HAD TAUGHT THE DISCIples the *Our Father*. He now gives them an even shorter version of the prayer, to help them to understand the former one. He omits the words, *Thy will be done*, to show that for God's kingdom to come fully in heaven and on earth is for men and angels to do His will. He omits the words *Deliver us from evil*, to show that only incurring debts toward God by *sin* is an evil simply speaking. Yet the Church uses the longer version of the prayer, as being easier for people in general to understand.

vv. 5–8

What does the parable of the importunate man represent? We might assume that the person who knocks at the door represents man, and the person in bed represents God. Yet in that case, the parable would be unnecessarily complicated: why introduce a third party, newly arrived from a journey? And why specify *three loaves*?

Who, then, are the three friends? In the previous chapter, our Saviour spoke of Himself as a Samaritan *on his journey*. Is He therefore, in this parable, the *friend* who has now *come off his journey*, by ascending into heaven? If so, then the *friend* to whom He comes must be His own Father. But what refreshment does the Father wish to set before His beloved Son, if not the faith, hope and charity of those for whom the Son died, as it were three loaves? For these will be the proof that Christ's work on earth was not in vain.

If so, it is the Father who knocks at our *door*, soliciting our attention through His graces, and it is we who reply *from within, Trouble me not*. He comes to us *at midnight*, while we are in the darkness of this world, and seeks from us the acts of the supernatural life. Man, though, occupies himself with his own schemes, the *children* of his imagination, fearing to be discomforted by God's plans for him, like one unwilling to rise from his *bed*. Yet God, by a kind *importunity*, will often disturb these schemes, not allowing

9 And I say to you, Ask, and it shall be given you: seek, and you shall find: knock, and it shall be opened to you.

10 For everyone that asketh, receiveth; and he that seeketh, findeth; and to him that knocketh, it shall be opened.

11 And which of you, if he ask his father bread, will he give him a stone? or a fish, will he for a fish give him a serpent?

12 Or if he shall ask an egg, will he reach him a scorpion?

13 If you then, being evil, know how to give good gifts to your children, how much more will your Father from heaven give the good Spirit to them that ask him?

14 And he was casting out a devil, and the same was dumb: and when he had cast out the devil, the dumb spoke: and the multitudes were in admiration at it:

15 But some of them said: He casteth out devils by Beelzebub, the prince of devils.

16 And others tempting, asked of him a sign from heaven.

17 But he seeing their thoughts, said to them: Every kingdom divided against itself, shall be brought to desolation, and house upon house shall fall.

18 And if Satan also be divided against himself, how shall his kingdom stand? because you say, that through Beelzebub I cast out devils.

19 Now if I cast out devils by Beelzebub; by whom do your children cast them out? Therefore they shall be your judges.

20 But if I by the finger of God cast out devils; doubtless the kingdom of God is come upon you.

them to succeed; and *if* God *shall continue knocking* by His grace, man begins to answer His call, not at first *because he is his friend*, but because he can now see nothing else to do. Yet Christ does not promise that His Father will continue to knock forever.

vv. 9–13

If God, the sovereign of creation, perseveres thus in asking help from His creatures, how much more fitting is it that we, who of ourselves are nothing, persevere in asking help from Him? As God asks for our acts of faith, hope and love, so we must *ask* from Him the power to produce these acts, since they surpass the resources of nature. We must ask for the *bread*, the *fish*, and the *egg*.

Bread may stand here for charity, nourished by the Bread of the Eucharist. Without this virtue, the heart is like a *stone*. Faith may be compared to a fish, since it believes in things unseen, like a fish hidden in the waters, and since it is attacked by the lies of the *serpent*. Our hope comes from the resurrection, when Life burst from the tomb as from an egg, and it looks forward to our own resurrection: therefore it is contrasted with the *scorpion*, which brings evil in its tail, since the man who hopes only for temporal things will be stung with anguish when his life ends.

vv. 14–26

Are the demons united or *divided*? They have a certain unity, since they agree in seeking the damnation of men, and because *Satan* imposes his will on the rest, which is why Christ can give the name of the principal fallen spirit to the whole mass of them. Yet each one seeks this end simply to satisfy his private malice: there is nothing that they love in common, as the blessed love God. For as long as this world lasts, therefore, the demons conceal their divisions: when there is no more opportunity to tempt mankind, they will turn upon each other, *and house upon house shall fall*.

Having indicated that the enemy is not yet divided, and lest His hearers conclude that the enemy's power will last indefinitely, Christ foretells His own despoliation of *the strong man*. By the fall of Adam, the devil made the whole human race *his spoils*. The devil also trusts in *his armour*, namely, the temptations behind

101

21 When a strong man armed keepeth his court, those things are in peace which he possesseth.

22 But if a stronger than he come upon him and overcome him; he will take away all his armour wherein he trusted, and will distribute his spoils.

23 He that is not with me, is against me; and he that gathereth not with me, scattereth.

24 When the unclean spirit is gone out of a man, he walketh through places without water, seeking rest; and not finding, he saith: I will return into my house whence I came out.

25 And when he is come, he findeth it swept and garnished.

26 Then he goeth and taketh with him seven other spirits more wicked than himself, and entering in, they dwell there. And the last state of that man becomes worse than the first.

27 And it came to pass, as he spoke these things, a certain woman from the crowd, lifting up her voice, said to him: Blessed is the womb that bore thee, and the paps that gave thee suck.

28 But he said: Yea rather, blessed are they who hear the word of God, and keep it.

which he hides and which he supposes will make it impossible for any man to *overcome him.* Christ will reveal the devil for who he is and *distribute his spoils* when He assigns to the just souls currently in *Sheol* the heavenly mansions prepared for them.

He then warns those who had accused Him of being in league with *Beelzebub,* that they themselves, though lacking the obvious signs of possession, are dangerously liable, at least, to demonic attack by reason of their ingratitude. Israel had been as it were exorcised by God, when He separated it from the pagans, whose gods are demons. But those who now reject the divine Exorcist come among them in person invite a demonic attack *worse* than those which the pagans suffer. If in addition they are also *swept and garnished,* that is, outwardly correct in their religion, they will only entice the enemy the more, who will be glad thus to express his contempt for the ancient law.

Since the devil sought to claim divine equality, God punishes his pride by subjecting him to material things. Here we learn that a common penalty for possessing a human being is to be sent *through places without water.* Such places pain the demon, both because it is humiliating for a pure spirit to be thus constrained in his movements, and because their aridity reminds him of the grace that he forsook in the beginning.

vv. 26–28

As on a previous occasion, Christ turns the attention of *the crowd* from His mother, knowing that this is what her humility desires, and teaches them all how they may become *blessed.* Yet the *woman* spoke the truth: to be mother of God is the greatest privilege that can be given to a human being. Therefore, our Lord, in a veiled way, also accepts and even augments the praise. Mary, more than anyone, has been able to *hear the word of God* in Person, having lived with Him from His conception, and even *to keep,* or guard, Him, for example during the flight into Egypt. Therefore also, the Church, *lifting up her voice* like the woman, uses this passage in the Mass of Saturday in honour of the Blessed Virgin.[1]

---

1 It is also used in the *Sacrosanctae,* a prayer traditionally said by clergy and religious at the end of the day to repair faults in the recitation of the divine office.

29 And the multitudes running together, he began to say: This generation is a wicked generation: it asketh a sign, and a sign shall not be given it, but the sign of Jonas the prophet.

30 For as Jonas was a sign to the Ninivites; so shall the Son of man also be to this generation.

31 The queen of the south shall rise in the judgment with the men of this generation and shall condemn them: because she came from the ends of the earth to hear the wisdom of Solomon; and behold more than Solomon here.

32 The men of Ninive shall rise in the judgment with this generation and shall

condemn it; because they did penance at the preaching of Jonas; and behold more than Jonas here.

33 No man lighteth a candle, and putteth it in a hidden place, nore under a bushel; but upon a candlestick, that they that come in, may see the light.

34 The light of thy body is thy eye. If thy eye be single, thy whole body will be lightsome: but if it be evil, thy body also will be darksome.

35 Take heed therefore, that the light which is in thee, be not darkness.

36 If then thy whole body be lightsome, having no part of darkness; the whole shall be lightsome; and as a bright lamp, shall enlighten thee.

37 And as he was speaking, a certain Pharisee prayed him, that he would dine with him. And he going in, sat down to eat.

38 And the Pharisee began to say, thinking within himself, why he was not washed before dinner.

39 And the Lord said to him: Now you Pharisees make clean the outside of the cup and of the platter; but your

inside is full of rapine and iniquity.

40 Ye fools, did not he that made that which is without, make also that which is within?

41 But yet that which remaineth, give alms; and behold, all things are clean unto you.

42 But woe to you, Pharisees, because you tithe mint and rue and every herb; and pass

vv. 29–36

After the interruption, He continues to warn His fellow countrymen that if they do not receive Him, they will end in a worse state than that of the pagans, especially since the conversion of *the queen of the South* and of *the men of Ninive* foreshadowed a future conversion of the nations. The Father has lit *a candle* in Israel for the Jews by sending His Son in the flesh, and He will not allow this candle to remain in the *hidden place* of the tomb, nor to be measured by human thinking, at it were placed *under a bushel*. By the resurrection and ascension, the Father will place His Son on high, as *upon a candlestick*, and the nations will see Him and *do penance*.

Yet some of the hearers might say to Christ, "If you are like a candle, how is it that we do not see?" It is because their *eye*, that is, their intention, is not *single*: they want to see a *sign* that will reveal their Messias to them, but only if it reveals one who corresponds to their worldly hopes. Just as a man's whole *body* might as well be in the dark if he has no eye to see, so if he darkens *the light* of his reason by such double-mindedness, the *whole body* of his thoughts and affections will remain unenlightened. On the other hand, if he desires only the truth then this body of thoughts and affections grows *lightsome*, and it will make *the whole* of his life to be *lightsome* too: he will see his way forwards, having now become *as a bright lamp*, and will recognise and confess Jesus as the Messias.

vv. 37–54

As we may infer from the end of this chapter, the invitation to dine was not made in a good spirit, but from a desire to hear something about which *they might accuse him*. However, the Lord does not address His words directly to His host, lest He seem to violate the duties of a guest, but rather to the whole company of Pharisees and scribes. They were fastidious about cleaning *cup and platter*, beyond what was prescribed by the Law, lest these vessels should come into contact with some ritually unclean person or animal. Our Lord uses these vessels as a symbol for man, who has both an external and an internal life. His hearers need cleansing from evil desires and plans, but have grown so hard-hearted that the only hope *that remaineth* for their conversion is for them to

over judgment, and the charity of God. Now these things you ought to have done, and not to leave the other undone.

43 Woe to you, Pharisees, because you love the uppermost seats in the synagogues, and salutations in the marketplace.

44 Woe to you, because you are as sepulchres that appear not, and men that walk over are not aware.

45 And one of the lawyers answering, saith to him: Master, in saying these things, thou reproachest us also.

46 But he said: Woe to you lawyers also, because you load men with burdens which they cannot bear, and you yourselves touch not the packs with one of your fingers.

47 Woe to you who build the monuments of the prophets: and your fathers killed them.

48 Truly you bear witness that you consent to the doings of your fathers: for they indeed killed them, and you build their sepulchres.

49 For this cause also the wisdom of God said: I will send to them prophets and apostles; and some of them they will kill and persecute.

50 That the blood of all the prophets which was shed from the foundation of the world, may be required of this generation,

51 From the blood of Abel unto the blood of Zacharias, who was slain between the alter and the temple: Yea I say to you, it shall be required of this generation.

52 Woe to you lawyers, for you have taken away the key of knowledge: you yourselves have not entered in, and those that were entering in, you have hindered.

53 And as he was saying these things to them, the Pharisees and the lawyers began violently to urge him, and to oppress his mouth about many things,

54 Lying in wait for him, and seeking to catch something from his mouth, that they might accuse him.

begin to give alms. For a wealthy man this is the least demanding of good works, but it opens a door to divine grace which can finish by making *all things clean unto* them, that is, bringing them to a state where none of their actions will now defile their souls.

Christ's words can also be translated: "That which is within, give as alms". This could mean "that which is within cup and platter", that is, give of your superfluous food to the poor; or also "that which is within you", that is, put your ingenuity and determination at their service.

At the end of His life, our Lord pronounces seven woes against the scribes and Pharisees. Here, as if to show that there is still a little time *that remaineth*, He pronounces six, the number of incompletion.

They are *as sepulchres that appear not*, since their impurity is not apparent, being moral and not ritual.

With irony, He speaks of the lawyers as completing the work of those who *killed the prophets*, by the building of those prophets' *sepulchres*.

Since He wishes to reveal His divinity gradually, He speaks of Himself now in the third person as *the wisdom of God*, who says: *I will send to them prophets*. Later, when pronouncing the seven woes, He will say simply: *I send to you prophets*.

Why is the blood of *all the prophets* from past days required of *this* one *generation*? Whatever grace was given to those prophets is present more abundantly in Christ, the head of the just, as in its source. Hence, to kill the Word incarnate is a graver sin than if this generation had killed all the prophets who had ever received the word of God. In this sense, even their punishment is a mercy, since it is less than their desert.

The Zacharias who was killed by order of King Joas was not the last martyr of Old Testament times. But the later martyrs of whom Scriptures speaks were killed by pagans, not by those who occupied positions of authority in God's people.

The *key of knowledge* seems to be the Old Testament, the correct interpretation of which would allow the people to welcome their Messias.

1 And when great multitudes stood about him, so that they trod one upon another, he began to say to his disciples: Beware ye of the leaven of the Pharisees, which is hypocrisy.

2 For there is nothing covered, that shall not be revealed: nor hidden, that shall not be known.

3 For whatsoever things you have spoken in darkness, shall be published in the light: and that which you have spoken in the ear in the chambers, shall be preached on the housetops.

4 And I say to you, my friends: Be not afraid of them who kill the body, and after that have no more that they can do.

5 But I will shew you whom you shall fear: fear ye him, who after he hath killed, hath power to cast into hell. Yea, I say to you, fear him.

6 Are not five sparrows sold for two farthings, and not one of them is forgotten before God?

7 Yea, the very hairs of your head are all numbered. Fear not therefore: you are of more value than many sparrows.

8 And I say to you, Whosoever shall confess me before men, him shall the Son of man confess me before men, him shall the Son of man also confess before the angels of God.

9 But he that shall deny me before men, shall be denied before the angels of God.

10 And whosoever speaketh a word against the Son of man, it shall be forgiven him: but to him that shall blaspheme against the Holy Ghost, it shall not be forgiven.

11 And when they shall bring you into the synagogues, and to magistrates and powers, be not solicitous how or what you shall answer, or what you shall say;

12 For the Holy Ghost shall teach you in the same hour what you must say.

COMMENTARY

VV. 1–12

SINCE SO MANY PEOPLE ARE COMING TO our Lord that *they trod one upon another*, it is time to warn the disciples against hypocrisy: seeing themselves revered as spiritual guides, they are in danger of believing themselves exempt from the ordinary duties of men. He therefore reminds them that all their sins will be *published in the light* of the last day. Since they are preachers, He speaks especially of sins of speech, warning them against the desire for temporal things, which leads both to words *spoken in the ear in the chambers,* that is to intrigue and flattery, and to guilty silence, owing to *fear* of those who can take such things from us. Fear of God, who can *cast into hell*, is the first remedy.

So that those who fail from fear to preach the gospel may not fall into despair, Christ says that any who speak *against the Son of man*, will *be forgiven* if they repent; yet not if they remain impenitent, which is the *sin against the Holy Ghost.*

13 And one of the multitude said to him: Master, speak to my brother that he divide the inheritance with me.

14 But he said to him: Man, who hath appointed me judge, or divider, over you?

15 And he said to them: Take heed and beware of all covetousness; for a man's life doth not consist in the abundance of things which he possesseth.

16 And he spoke a similitude to them, saying: The land of a certain rich man brought forth plenty of fruits.

17 And he thought within himself, saying: What shall I do, because I have no room where to bestow my fruits?

18 And he said: This will I do: I will pull down my barns, and will build greater; and into them will I gather all things that are grown to me, and my goods.

19 And I will say to my soul: Soul, thou hast much goods laid up for many years; take thy rest; eat, drink, make good cheer.

20 But God said to him: Thou fool, this night do they require thy soul of thee: and whose shall those things be which thou hast provided?

21 So is he that layeth up treasure for himself and is not rich towards God.

22 And he said to his disciples: Therefore I say to you, be not solicitous for your life, what you shall eat; nor for your body, what you shall put on.

23 The life is more than the meat, and the body is more than the raiment.

24 Consider the ravens, for they sow not, neither do they reap, neither have they storehouse nor barn, and God feedeth them. How much are you more valuable than they?

25 And which of you, by taking thought, can add to his stature one cubit?

26 If then ye be not able to do so much as the least thing, why are you solicitous for the rest?

27 Consider the lilies, how they grow: they labour not, neither do they spin. But I say to you, not even Solomon in all his glory was clothed like one of these.

28 Now if God clothe in this manner the grass that is today in the field, and tomorrow is cast into the oven, how much more you, O ye of little faith?

vv. 13–34

The question: *Man, who hath appointed me judge, or divider, over you*, has a double meaning. The more obvious sense is that Jesus has not come into the world to exercise temporal power, such as is exercised by kings or judges, even though He had the right to do so. The deeper sense is that it is the eternal Father who *hath appointed* him the *judge* of mankind, and the *divider* of the wicked from the just; when Christ's interlocutor reflects on that, he will less desire to burden himself with riches. Our Lord warns not only against covetousness but against *all covetousness*: for one may desire in a disordered way to have an *abundance* not only of material goods but also of learning or even of 'experiences'.

Who are *they* who *require* the *soul* of the rich fool? Perhaps the demons; or else the angels, to bring the soul before the throne of God. The one who is *rich towards God*, by contrast, places his *fruits* in the *barns* of God, that is, in a treasury of merit that will be waiting for him when he leaves this life, and that can also benefit other souls. By saying *where your treasure is, there will your heart be also*, Christ shows the reality of this merit. Otherwise, the saying would only mean "your heart is wherever the thing that is dear to you is", which would be to say little. The more we merit heaven, the more we shall desire it.

The second remedy to disordered desire for temporal things is lively faith in divine providence, which governs even the *sparrows*.[1] What of the objection that necessities are sometimes lacking? We do not often hear of the servants of God perishing for want of *meat* or *raiment*, but if it happens, they know that this is for them the way to the eternal good, to which no one can come but though some kind of death.

---

1 From this chapter we learn that Palestinian merchants, like our own, sought for custom by special offers. St Matthew tells us that *two sparrows are sold for a farthing*, and here we find that *five sparrows are sold for two farthings*.

29 And seek not what you shall eat, or what you shall drink: and be not lifted up on high.

30 For all these things do the nations of the world seek. But your Father knoweth that you have need of these things.

31 But seek ye first the kingdom of God and his justice, and all these things shall be added unto you.

35 Let your loins be girt, and lamps burning in your hands.

36 And you yourselves like to men who wait for their lord, when he shall return from the wedding; that when he cometh and knocketh, they may open to him immediately.

37 Blessed are those servants, whom the Lord when he cometh, shall find watching. Amen I say to you, that he will gird himself, and make them sit down to meat, and

32 Fear not, little flock, for it hath pleased your Father to give you a kingdom.

33 Sell what you possess and give alms. Make to yourselves bags which grow not old, a treasure in heaven which faileth not: where no thief approacheth, nor moth corrupteth.

34 For where your treasure is, there will your heart be also.

passing will minister unto them.

38 And if he shall come in the second watch, or come in the third watch, and find them so, blessed are those servants.

39 But this know ye, that if the householder did know at what hour the thief would come, he would surely watch, and would not suffer his house to be broken open.

40 Be you then also ready: for at what hour you think not, the Son of man will come.

vv. 35–40

A final remedy against cares and earthly desires is to remember that the hour of death, which will render them all vain, is uncertain. Our Lord therefore tells the disciples that at their death, He will as it were *return from the wedding* now being celebrated in heaven, and assign to each what is due for his ministry in the Church. He will *come in the second watch* of the night *or in the third,* but not in the final, fourth watch, since He comes for individual souls now sooner, now later, but while the night of this world is continuing.

He will make them sit down to meat, since He will feed the saints with the vision of the Blessed Trinity, *and passing will minister unto them,* since He will do the will of those who did His will on earth.

As well as the *Lord,* there is also a *thief* and a *householder* or *steward.* The thief is the devil, or antichrist, who will steal the honour due to the Lord. The steward or householder is the chief of the servants, and represents the bishop of each church, and especially the bishop of Rome. They have not been told when antichrist will come. Yet how can the same person be both householder and also servant or steward? We are to think of a bishop in the first way, because of his authority, but he is to think of himself in the second way, since he must give account of how he uses it. [2]

---

2 In Luke 13:25, however, the Greek word translated here as 'householder'

41 And Peter said to him: Lord, dost thou speak this parable to us, or likewise to all?

42 And the Lord said: Who (thinkest thou) is the faithful and wise steward, whom his lord setteth over his family, to give them their measure of wheat in due season?

43 Blessed is that servant, whom when his lord shall come, he shall find so doing.

44 Verily I say to you, he will set him over all that he possesseth.

45 But if that servant shall say in his heart: My lord is long a coming; and shall begin to strike the menservants and maidservants, and to eat and to drink and be drunk:

46 The lord of that servant will come in the day that he hopeth not, and at the hour that he knoweth not, and shall separate him, and shall appoint him his portion with unbelievers.

47 And that servant who knew the will of his lord, and prepared not himself, and did not according to his will, shall be beaten with many stripes.

48 But he that knew not, and did things worthy of stripes, shall be beaten with few stripes. And unto whomsoever much is given, of him much shall be required: and to whom they have committed much, of him they will demand the more.

49 I am come to cast fire on the earth; and what will I, but that it be kindled?

50 And I have a baptism wherewith I am to be baptized: and how am I straitened until it be accomplished?

51 Think ye, that I am come to give peace on earth? I tell you, no; but separation.

52 For there shall be from henceforth five in one house divided: three against two, and two against three.

53 The father shall be divided against the son, and the son against his father, the mother against the daughter, and the daughter against the mother, the mother in law against her daughter in law, and the daughter in law against her mother in law.

54 And he said also to the multitudes: When you see a cloud rising from the west, presently you say: A shower is coming: and so it happeneth:

55 And when ye see the south wind blow, you say: There will be heat: and it cometh to pass.

vv. 41–48

St Peter wonders whether Christ is speaking of His coming back simply to the existing group of disciples. In His reply, our Lord suggests the long line of Peter's successors, some good and some bad, that will endure to His return. The faithful ones *will* be *set over all that* Christ *possesseth*, which suggests that every pope who enters heaven is made a patron of the universal Church. But Christ will *separate* the unfaithful pope from communion with Himself for eternity. The Greek word that comes into English as 'separate' is a violent one, often translated as 'cut in two': it suggests the unnatural state of a pope severed from the honour of the papacy and cast into hell, *with unbelievers.*

Other clergy may be *beaten with many* or *with few stripes* at their judgement, which suggests different degrees of punishment in hell or else a longer or shorter period in purgatory. Ignorance of the will of Christ will be a mitigating factor, but not an exculpating one, since the Lord makes it possible for the clergy to know His will if they seek it.

vv. 49–59

In contrast with this universal Church that He will found, Jesus is for now as it were *straitened*, the *fire* of His charity being confined within Palestine. Yet, though both the Gentiles and the Jews will be invited into this Church, *peace* between them will not immediately result. Though God wishes the world to be but *one house*, yet the old Law, in those who will continue to practise it, and the Synagogue, as *father* and *mother*, will be *divided* against their *Son*, Jesus, and against their *daughter*, Mary, and against their *daughter-in-law*, each faithful soul.

To prevent this as far as possible, He bids the *multitudes* to *discern the time*, and to recognise from *the face of the heaven*, that is,

---

must refer to Christ Himself. This suggests the teaching of Pope Boniface VIII in *Unam sanctam*, that Christ and His vicar are not to be thought of as two heads of the mystical body: the pope, when he acts as pope, exercises the one headship of Christ over the Church.

56 You hypocrites, you know how to discern the face of the heaven and of the earth: but how is it that you do not discern this time?

57 And why even of yourselves, do you not judge that which is just?

58 And when thou goest with thy adversary to the prince, whilst thou art in the way, endeavour to be delivered from him: lest perhaps he draw thee to the judge, and the judge deliver thee to the exacter, and the exacter cast thee into prison.

59 I say to thee, thou shalt not go out thence, until thou pay the very last mite.

from Holy Scripture, *and of the earth*, that is, from what they see happening around them, that their Messias is here. If only from self-interest, they should want to *judge* what the *just* response is to His preaching and miracles. He sees that their minds are weighed down by the burden of their sins, as if by an *adversary*, as they make their *way* through this life to the *prince* or ruler, God the Father, who has appointed Jesus as *judge*. Unless they are *delivered* from this burden by lively faith, Christ must *deliver* them to the *exactor*, the angel appointed to lead souls to the *prison* either of purgatory or of hell, depending on whether or not they depart this life in a state of grace. In either case, they will have to stay until they *pay the very last* of their debt, which in the case of hell would mean staying for ever, since the lost souls will never desire to pay it.

1 And there were present, at that very time, some that told him of the Galileans, whose blood Pilate had mingled with their sacrifices.

2 And he answering, said to them: Think you that these Galileans were sinners above all the men of Galilee, because they suffered such things?

3 No, I say to you: but unless you shall do penance, you shall all likewise perish.

4 Or those eighteen upon whom the tower fell in Siloe, and slew them: think you, that they also were debtors above all the men that dwelt in Jerusalem?

5 No, I say to you; but except you do penance, you shall all likewise perish.

6 He spoke also this parable: A certain man had a fig tree planted in his vineyard, and he came seeking fruit on it, and found none.

7 And he said to the dresser of the vineyard: Behold, for these three years I come seeking fruit on this fig tree, and I find none. Cut it done therefore: why cumbereth it the ground?

8 But he answering, said to him: Lord, let it alone this year also, until I dig about it, and dung it.

9 And if happily it bear fruit: but if not, then after that thou shalt cut it down.

10 And he was teaching in their synagogue on their sabbath.

11 And behold there was a woman, who had a spirit of infirmity eighteen years: and she was bowed together,

vv. 1–5

SINCE THIS CHAPTER BEGINS *AT THAT VERY time* when our Lord was bidding His hearers recognise the fulfilment of the prophecies about the Messias, we can expect His words here to continue this theme. He does not commend those *Galileans* who sought a temporal deliverance from Roman rule; those who do not *do penance* for the sins that incline men to hope for such a Messias will *perish*, that is, fail to obtain eternal life. Lest He seem to slight His fellow Galileans, He then speaks of some Judaeans. *Siloe*, as St John tells us, means 'sent', or the one sent, and it is in Jerusalem.[1] The *tower* of the one who is sent could thus mean the prophecies of the Old Testament, by which Christ, could be seen from afar, as from a tower, even before He was sent by the Father. This tower *fell and slew* those inside when those to whom the prophecies belonged by right failed to recognise their fulfilment.

The number eighteen recurs in the first part of this chapter. In Greek, this number corresponds to the letters *Iota* plus *Eta*, which are the first two letters of the name *Jesus*. Eighteen is therefore taken by some of the Fathers as a symbol of Christ.

vv. 6–21

The Lord knows that Israel as a whole will remain for a long time without faith in Him. They will be like *a fig tree planted in his vineyard*, that is, intended to bear *fruit* in His Church, and not doing so. He will come *seeking* it *for three years*, which suggests the time of His public ministry. As once to Moses, the Lord threatens to blot out this people, asking why it *cumbereth the ground*, that is, why it receives a disproportionate degree of attention from God's ministers. The *dresser of the vineyard*, perhaps the patron of the universal Church, intercedes for Israel, that it be *let alone also* during the acceptable *year* of the new covenant, asking *to dig about it and dung it*, that it may be separated from

---

1 Jn. 9:7.

neither could she look upwards at all.

12 Whom when Jesus saw, he called her unto him, and said to her: Woman, thou art delivered from thy infirmity.

13 And he laid his hands upon her, and immediately she was made straight, and glorified God.

14 And the ruler of the synagogue (being angry that Jesus had healed on the sabbath) answering, said to the multitude: Six days there are wherein you ought to work. In them therefore come, and be healed; and not on the sabbath day.

15 And the Lord answering him, said: Ye hypocrites, doth not every one of you, on the sabbath day, loose his ox or his ass from the manger, and lead them to water?

16 And ought not this daughter of Abraham, whom Satan

hath bound, lo, these eighteen years, be loosed from this bond on the sabbath day?

17 And when he said these things, all his adversaries were ashamed: and all the people rejoiced for all the things that were gloriously done by him.

18 He said therefore: To what is the kingdom of God like, and whereunto shall I resemble it?

19 It is like to a grain of mustard seed, which a man took and cast into his garden, and it grew and became a great tree, and the birds of the air lodged in the branches thereof.

20 And again he said: Whereunto shall I esteem the kingdom of God to be like?

21 It is like to leaven, which a woman took and hid in three measures of meal, till the whole was leavened.

22 And he went through the cities and towns teaching, and making his journey to Jerusalem.

23 And a certain man said to him: Lord, are they few that are saved? But he said to them:

24 Strive to enter by the narrow gate; for many, I say to you,

shall seek to enter, and shall not be able.

25 But when the master of the house shall be gone in, and shall shut the door, you shall begin to stand without, and knock at the door, saying: Lord, open to us. And he answering, shall

the rest of men and covered with opprobrium, in the hope that it will then *bear fruit*.

This parable is illustrated by a healing. The *daughter of Abraham,* suffering *eighteen years* of *infirmity*, represents the Israel that would suffer from its rejection of Jesus, and be unable to *look upwards*, by believing in the resurrection and ascension of Christ, until it is *loosed.*

The people *rejoice* at the miracles that He *gloriously* accomplishes. *Therefore,* lest they take scandal later at the Cross, He proposes two parables that teach that humility is of the essence of the gospel. By His incarnation, the Word was as it were *cast* like a *mustard-seed* into the Father's *garden*. During His earthly life, our Lord was apparently unimportant: He did not have money at His disposal or people at His command. At His resurrection, He *grew and became a great tree,* the head and principle of the Church.

Yet there is also a *woman* who co-operates in this. *Leaven,* which makes flour seem to live, represents graces of the Holy Spirit, the Life-giver. And Mary, by her compassion on earth and her prayer in heaven, becomes the 'dispensatrix' of all the graces by which the *three measures of* flour, Christians in heaven, earth, and purgatory are *leavened*, so as to become Christ, the bread of life.

vv. 22–30

Our Lord does not tell His questioner what proportion of mankind the *saved* will be, as it would not have profited him to know it. But He tells him that *many* will fail *to enter*. After death, such people will *knock at the door* in that they will retain their natural desire for happiness, even though they will reject heaven by their free will. Among them will be some who will have *eaten and drunk* the mysteries of Christ's real *presence*, and heard His words *taught*. As some Jews will *see*, from the outside, *Abraham, Isaac and Jacob in the kingdom of God*, so some Catholics

say to you: I know you not, whence you are.

26 Then you shall begin to say: We have eaten and drunk in thy presence, and thou hast taught in our streets.

27 And he shall say to you: I know you not, whence you are: depart from me, all ye workers of iniquity.

28 There shall be weeping and gnashing of teeth, when you shall see Abraham and Isaac and Jacob, and all the prophets, in the kingdom of God, and you yourselves thrust out.

29 And there shall come from the east and the west, and the north and the south; and shall sit down in the kingdom of God.

30 And behold, they are last that shall be first; and they are first that shall be last.

31 The same day, there came some of the Pharisees, saying to him: Depart, and get thee hence, for Herod hath a mind to kill thee.

32 And he said to them: Go and tell that fox, Behold, I cast out devils, and do cures today and tomorrow, and the third day I am consummated.

33 Nevertheless I must walk today and tomorrow, and the day following, because it cannot be that a prophet perish out of Jerusalem.

34 Jerusalem, Jerusalem, that killest the prophets, and stonest them that are sent to thee, how often would I have gathered thy children as the bird doth her brood under her wings, and thou wouldest not?

35 Behold your house shall be left to you desolate. And I say to you, that you shall not see me till the time come, when you shall say: Blessed is he that cometh in the name of the Lord.

will see saints whose names were familiar to them on earth, but whose lives they did not imitate.

vv. 31–33

His reply to the *Pharisees* has two meanings. More simply, that He will continue His earthly mission without being deflected, till it is *consummated* in death. The hidden meaning is that He will continue His mission even *tomorrow*, that is, beyond death, delivering the just in the underworld from the power of the *devils*, and bringing *cures* to their remaining infirmities, and then will rise again *the third day.*

vv. 34–35

He returns sorrowfully to the long wait that Israel will have to endure because of its unbelief. The *house* of the temple will be made *desolate* of the divine presence, and the Jews will *not see* their Lord again until they find this presence beneath the Eucharistic species and say in the words of the liturgy: *Blessed is he that cometh in the name of the Lord.* [2]

---

2 These words are used, for example, in the liturgy of St John Chrysostom and the liturgy of St James, as well as in the Roman Mass.

1 And it came to pass, when Jesus went into the house of one of the chief of the Pharisees, on the sabbath day, to eat bread, that they watched him.

2 And behold, there was a certain man before him that had the dropsy.

3 And Jesus answering, spoke to the lawyers and Pharisees, saying: Is it lawful to heal on the sabbath day?

4 But they held their peace. But he taking him, healed him, and sent him away.

5 And answering them, he said: Which of you shall have an ass or an ox fall into a pit, and will not immediately draw him out, on the sabbath day?

6 And they could not answer him to these things.

7 And he spoke a parable also to them that were invited, marking how they chose the first seats at the table, saying to them:

8 When thou art invited to a wedding, sit not down in the first place, lest perhaps one more honourable than thou be invited by him:

9 And he that invited thee and him, come and say to thee, Give this man place: and then thou begin with shame to take the lowest place.

10 But when thou art invited, go, sit down in the lowest place; that when he who invited thee, cometh, he may say to thee: Friend, go up higher. Then shalt thou have glory before them that sit at table with thee.

11 Because everyone that exalteth himself, shall be humbled; and he that humbleth himself, shall be exalted.

VV. 1–11

THE ATMOSPHERE IS TENSE. A *SABBATH* meal should have been a festive occasion, but instead: *They were watching him.* The situation deteriorates when Christ first asks them a question which they are afraid to answer, then heals the man with *dropsy*, that is, severe water-retention, and finally by a question shows that their interpretation of the Law is inconsistent and inhuman. They will free their own valuable *beast* on the Sabbath day, dragging it even with great effort from the water or mud in which it is stuck, so how can they object if He frees a man made in God's image from the water that is making his life miserable?

Perhaps in response to this hostile atmosphere, our Lord goes on to tell a *parable*. If the minds of the Pharisee and his friends can be turned to searching out the meaning of a riddle, then at least they will no longer be occupied with their grievance against Him.

It must have been clear at least to the more intelligent of our Lord's hearers that He is not really interested in telling them how to obtain for themselves the maximum amount of *glory* at a *wedding*. If He had really been thinking about human honour, He would have had no reason to limit His advice to wedding-banquets, since the technique of sitting *in the lowest place* in order to be brought higher would work equally well on all occasions.

The wedding is Christ's favourite image for the communion to which the Blessed Trinity calls all rational beings. The first to be invited were the angels. By a single act of submission to the divine will, they had the power to enter into beatitude. Yet Lucifer refused to obey. He desired to have a position that belongs to God alone: to possess beatitude as if by right, not as a gift and as a reward for obedience. He thus put himself, at least by desire, *in the first place*, and so he was thrown from heaven, and began *with shame to take the lowest* one, kept in darkness, says St Peter, till the day of judgement.

12 And he said to him also that had invited him: When thou makest a dinner or a supper, call not thy friends, nor thy brethren, nor thy kinsmen, nor thy neighbours who are rich; lest perhaps they also invite thee again, and a recompense be made to thee.

13 But when thou makest a feast, call the poor, the maimed, the lame, and the blind;

14 And thou shalt be blessed, because they have not wherewith to make thee recompense: for recompense shall be made thee at the resurrection of the just.

Lucifer was by nature an angel of great beauty, perhaps the highest of all, and yet the Father had *invited one more honourable than* him to enter creation. Jesus of Nazareth is the Word of God in person, and therefore beatitude does belong to Him by right. Therefore, when He became man, His human soul did not have to merit the beatific vision, but possessed it from the first moment. Yet He chose the womb of the Virgin, birth in a cave, exile in Egypt, obscurity in Nazareth. Though He was the Bridegroom, He acted as if He were a mere guest at His own wedding-banquet.

Then since He, the Son, became *humbler yet, even to accepting death, death on a Cross*, the Father as it were said to Him on the morning of His Resurrection, *My friend, come up higher.* By His ascension, Jesus obtained *the highest place, in the sight of all* the holy angels, as He will be manifested to absolutely all rational beings, elect and reprobate alike, on the last day.

The Pharisee and the other guests could hardly have grasped the deep meaning of this parable. But they could have understood the concluding law about the exaltation of the *humble*. God will ensure that those who persevere in humility will be honoured, not by powerful people in this world, which would be more a trial than a reward, but *by those who sit at table* with Him in the next.

He calls this wedding-banquet both *a dinner* and *a supper*: a dinner, since it takes place in the full light of glory, and a supper, since it comes after the labours of this life.

vv. 12–24

When people speak at table, they are usually in a relaxed mood. Perhaps this is why our Lord responds to the man's exclamation: *Blessed is he,* with a parable that warns that some of those *invited* will fail *to eat bread in the kingdom of God.*

The Word of the Father *invited many* to *a great supper*, the heavenly banquet. Only one *servant* calls mankind to it, to signify that the whole order of preachers must preach one gospel down the ages. There are three great obstacles to reaching it: the desire for power, signified by the purchase of the *farm*; the desire to

15 When one of them that sat at table with him, had heard these things, he said to him: Blessed is he that shall eat bread in the kingdom of God.

16 But he said to him: A certain man made a great supper and invited many.

17 And he sent his servant at the hour of supper to say to them that were invited that they should come, for now all things are ready.

18 And they began all at once to make excuse. The first said to him: I have bought a farm, and I must needs go out and see it: I pray thee, hold me excused.

19 And another said: I have bought five yoke of oxen, and I go to try them: I pray thee, hold me excused.

20 And another said: I have married a wife, and therefore I cannot come.

21 And the servant returning, told these things to his lord. Then the master of the house, being angry, said to his servant: Go out quickly into the streets and lanes of the city, and bring in hither the poor, and the feeble, and the blind, and the lame.

22 And the servant said: Lord, it is done as thou hast commanded, and yet there is room.

23 And the Lord said to the servant: Go out into the highways and hedges, and compel them to come in, that my house may be filled.

24 But I say unto you, that none of those men that were invited, shall taste of my supper.

25 And there went great multitudes with him. And turning, he said to them:

26 If any man come to me, and hate not his father, and mother, and wife, and children, and brethren, and sisters, yea and his own life also, he cannot be my disciple.

27 And whosoever doth not carry his cross and come after me, cannot be my disciple.

28 For which of you having a mind to build a tower, doth not first sit down, and reckon the charges that are necessary, whether he have wherewithal to finish it:

29 Lest, after he hath laid the foundation, and is not able to finish it, all that see it begin to mock him,

remain on the level of the senses, symbolised, St Augustine tells us, by *five yoke of oxen*, since all the senses are in a way double; and heresy, which resembles a domineering *wife*. This last causes the servant to be so despised that the one invited no longer even asks to *be excused*.

Those who are unimpressive in worldly terms are often readier to accept the invitation to beatitude, for what have they to lose?

But the preacher must not be content to speak to those in *the city*, for example to Catholics only, but must *go out into the highways*, to those who seem to be travelling in search of some truth, and even to *the hedges*, to those who sit idly and in stupor. He must *compel them to come in*, not by bodily force, which is alien to his calling and which none may employ to induce men to baptism, but by the power of his words and example.

vv. 25–35

Any crowd of people generates a kind of enthusiasm. But Christ knows that a merely natural enthusiasm for His fellowship will not be sufficient to overcome all trials. Hence, in proportion as His popularity grows, and *great multitudes* go *with him,* He warns them more expressly of the cost of being his *disciple*. The disciple must *hate* all that is naturally dearest to him, that is, be willing to *renounce* it, if it prove an obstacle to discipleship.

The Christian life, or the religious life, is compared to *a tower*, since it reaches to heaven. Before entering it, we are to *reckon* whether we *have wherewithal to finish*: not whether we already

30 Saying: This man began to build and was not able to finish.

31 Or what king, about to go to make war against another king, doth not first sit down, and think whether he be able, with ten thousand, to meet him that, with twenty thousand, cometh against him?

32 Or else, whilst the other is yet afar off, sending an embassy, he desireth conditions of peace.

33 So likewise every one of you that doth not renounce all that he possesseth, cannot be my disciple.

34 Salt is good. But if the salt shall lose its savour, wherewith shall it be seasoned?

35 It is neither profitable for the land nor for the dunghill, but shall be cast out. He that hath ears to hear, let him hear.

have the strength to do so, but whether we have the firm intention to seek this strength from God as we go along.

The Holy Ghost makes the baptised person a *king*, yet he must fight with only *ten thousand*, that is, with simplicity, against the *twenty thousand* of *another king*, that is, against the duplicity of the devil. Those who are unwilling to forsake the conveniences that sin can bring them will inevitably send *an embassy* to this enemy, bartering with the rights of God so that they may live in *peace*. But such a half-hearted Christian will be *neither profitable for the land*, bringing no good to the Church, *nor for the dunghill*, being distrusted by the world.

1 Now the publicans and sinners drew near unto him to hear him.

2 And the Pharisees and the scribes murmured, saying: This man receiveth sinners, and eateth with them.

3 And he spoke to them this parable, saying:

4 What man of you that hath an hundred sheep: and if he shall lose one of them, doth he not leave the ninety-nine in the desert, and go after that which was lost, until he find it?

5 And when he hath found it, lay it upon his shoulders, rejoicing:

6 And coming home, call together his friends and neighbours, saying to them: Rejoice with me, because I

have found my sheep that was lost?

7 I say to you, that even so there shall be joy in heaven upon one sinner that doth penance, more than upon ninety-nine just who need not penance.

8 Or what woman having ten groats; if she lose one groat, doth not light a candle, and sweep the house, and seek diligently until she find it?

9 And when she hath found it, call together her friends and neighbours, saying: Rejoice with me, because I have found the groat which I had lost.

10 So I say to you, there shall be joy before the angels of God upon one sinner doing penance.

VV. 1–10

HO ARE THE *NINETY-NINE* SHEEP IN THE *desert*? Perhaps the scribes and Pharisees themselves, since pride makes the soul a wilderness where no virtue may grow. Only *one* sheep is said to escape this pride, though still to wander about *lost*, since the Father's love for each soul is unique. The good shepherd places this sheep *upon his shoulders, rejoicing,* to show that He would gladly take up the Cross for the salvation of even one human being. Afterward, He does not return to the desert but to His heavenly *home*, bidding His *friends*, the Father and the Holy Ghost, *and neighbours*, the blessed spirits, *rejoice* at the accomplishment of the redemption.

With a divine irony, but also as an appeal to their conscience, our Lord speaks of the *ninety-nine* as *just*. Can the scribes and Pharisees suppose that, unlike Moses or David, they *need not penance*?

The next parable must have another meaning, or why would it be needed? If Christ is the good shepherd, who is the woman? Surely, the Blessed Virgin, since He has given her to mankind to make it easy for sinners to return to Him. She has only nine of her *ten groats*. Some spiritual authors see these as a symbol for the angelic orders, of which Sacred Scripture gives us nine names, with the human race making a tenth. Mary is queen of angels, but this is not enough for her while there are men still perishing. She wants to find the *one groat* that is missing. She is said to *light a candle*, since unlike Jesus, who always possessed the beatific vision, she acquired it by the merit of her life. As a woman by the light of a lamp may see the whole house — we should imagine it as a simple dwelling, like that of the holy family — so our Lady, by the light of glory, sees the whole race of men.

Is the comparison far-fetched? No, since our Lord finishes by speaking of the *joy* of the *angels* when the missing coin is found.

11 And he said: A certain man had two sons:

12 And the younger of them said to his father: Father, give me the portion of substance that falleth to me. And he divided unto them his substance.

13 And not many days after, the younger son, gathering all together, went abroad into a far country: and there wasted his substance, living riotously.

14 And after he had spent all, there came a mighty famine in that country; and he began to be in want.

15 And he went and cleaved to one of the citizens of that country. And he sent him into his farm to feed swine.

16 And he would fain have filled his belly with the husks the swine did eat; and no man gave unto him.

17 And returning to himself, he said: How many hired servants in my father's house abound with bread, and I here perish with hunger?

18 I will arise, and will go to my father, and say to him: Father, I have sinned against heaven, and before thee:

19 I am not worthy to be called thy son: make me as one of thy hired servants.

20 And rising up he came to his father. And when he was yet a great way off, his father saw him, and was moved with compassion, and running to him fell upon his neck, and kissed him.

21 And the son said to him: Father, I have sinned against heaven, and before thee, I am not now worthy to be called thy son.

22 And the father said to his servants: Bring forth quickly the first robe, and put it on him, and put a ring on his hand, and shoes on his feet:

23 And bring hither the fatted calf, and kill it, and let us eat and make merry:

24 Because this my son was dead, and is come to life again: was lost, and is found. And they began to be merry.

25 Now his elder son was in the field, and when he came and drew nigh to the house, he heard music and dancing:

26 And he called one of the servants and asked what these things meant.

27 And he said to him: Thy brother is come, and thy father hath killed the fatted calf, because he hath received him safe.

vv. 11–32

All human beings can be compared to the sons of God, since they bear the divine image. On coming to the age of reason, they inherit *the portion of substance that falleth to* them by nature, the power of free choice. *Not* long *after* this, most of them go *abroad into a far country* of unlikeness to God. Their *substance* is *wasted* by mortal sins, which weaken and remove the power of doing right, and they experience a *mighty famine* of the happiness that they had promised to themselves. Some demon or other, *one of the citizens of that country* of unlikeness, thereby gains power over them, forcing them now to *feed the swine* of their disordered desires, though they themselves gain no lasting satisfaction from it.

By an actual grace, such a person may return *to himself*, glimpsing his original dignity. Yet of himself, he cannot know that God is willing to forgive his sins, and make of him a *son* and a sharer in the divine nature. He can know and desire to fulfil his duty as a creature, yet he does not know whether even this desire will be acceptable, given his past sins. Hence, he does not even seek to become *one of* God's *servants,* but only to be *as* a servant.

While he remains *a great way off*, burdened with many mortal sins, God goes *to him*, sending new graces to strengthen his resolutions. If the person perseveres, he will be made just, God infusing into him the Holy Spirit, by whom the soul is as it were *kissed*, since the third divine Person is the expression of the charity that unites the Father and the Son. He is now clothed in *the first robe*, the sanctifying grace that Adam possessed before his fall, and receives the *ring on his hand* to show that his actions will now bear the seal of divine approval, and *shoes on his feet*, the power to mortify his passions. God will invite this soul to *make merry* at the death of the *fatted calf*, by a perpetual gratitude for the sacrifice of Christ.

Although the parable thus far applies to anyone who falls into sin and returns to God, it has often been understood to have a special application to the gentiles. They are the younger son who took their *portion of substance* from the Creator, when they used their gifts of intellect, bodily strength and imagination not for the worship of the true God but for *living riotously* in false

28 And he was angry, and would not go in. His father therefore coming out began to entreat him.

29 And he answering, said to his father: Behold, for so many years do I serve thee, and I have never transgressed thy commandment, and yet thou hast never given me a kid to make merry with my friends:

30 But as soon as this thy son is come, who hath devoured his substance with harlots, thou hast killed for him the fatted calf.

31 But he said to him: Son, thou art always with me, and all I have is thine.

32 But it was fit that we should make merry and be glad, for this thy brother was dead and is come to life again; he was lost and is found.

religions, arts, human philosophies and military exploits. By the time of the incarnation, they had experienced that all this left the *belly* of their soul empty. While they were in this state, Christ *was moved with compassion* for these *other sheep, not of the* Jewish *fold*, and sent His apostles, in whom He dwelt, *running* to them.

The elder son will then represent the Jewish people. At the preaching of the gospel, they *drew nigh to the house* of the Church, by seeing the gladness of the Gentile converts. From *one of the servants* of Christ preaching in the synagogues, they learn that the Creator had *received* the repentance of the nations. They grew *angry and would not go in*, reflecting how much they themselves had suffered, and how easy, it seemed, was the lot of the gentiles. They complain that God had never *given* them even *a kid to make merry*, since the temporal Messias they hoped for had not come. But this people are *always with* Him, being *most dear for the sake of their fathers*, and therefore He will *entreat* them to come in. *All* that He has is theirs, since spiritual gifts are not diminished when they are shared among many.

CHAPTER 16

1 And he said also to his disciples: There was a certain rich man who had a steward: and the same was accused unto him, that he had wasted his goods.

2 And he called him, and said to him: How is it that I hear this of thee? give an account of thy stewardship: for now thou canst be steward no longer.

vv. 1–9

THIS IS PROBABLY THE MOST DIFFICULT OF the parables, but one of the Fathers of the Church has given us a way to understand it.[1] It speaks of the relations between God, the devil, and mankind. The *rich man*, who owns all the property, stands for almighty God, who owns all things, having created them out of nothing, and who is also *rich in mercy*.

The *steward* represents the devil. Although the devil desires to frustrate God's plans as much as possible, nevertheless, God makes use of him. If a skilful composer can use even the most unpromising musical instrument to produce some special effect for a symphony, so God in His wisdom can make use even of a creature who is fixed in hostility against Him.

God therefore granted the devil a certain power over mankind, as a steward has a certain power in his master's estate. He was allowed to test our first parents. He induced the generation after the flood to build the tower of Babel. Later, among the chosen people, he tempted the high priest Aaron to give way to the people's demands for a visible god to worship, and thus the golden calf was made. Later still, he tempted King Solomon to go to excess in taking foreign wives, until Solomon fell from wisdom into folly, and began to worship idols. All this and much else God permitted, so that mankind might have experience of temptation, and so that resisting it, through His grace, they might merit an eternal reward.

Yet the devil, in his envy of the heavenly beatitude available to us, went beyond all bounds in his malice toward the human race. He *wasted* the rich man's *goods*. He induced countless human beings not only to sin against God's commandments, but also to embrace monstrous religions. He filled men's imaginations with unclean images, and their hearts with terror of unknown forces.

The Blessed Trinity therefore resolved to withdraw from the devil the power which he had held, saying to him: *Now thou*

---

1 St Gaudentius, bishop of Brescia. He lived in the 4th century, and was a friend of St Ambrose.

3 And the steward said within himself: What shall I do, because my lord taketh away from me the stewardship? To dig I am not able; to beg I am ashamed.

4 I know what I will do, that when I shall be removed from the stewardship, they may receive me into their houses.

5 Therefore calling together every one of his lord's debtors, he said to the first: How much dost thou owe my lord?

6 But he said: An hundred barrels of oil. And he said to him: Take thy bill and sit down quickly and write fifty.

7 Then he said to another: And how much dost thou owe? Who said: An hundred quarters of wheat. He said to him: Take thy bill and write eighty.

8 And the lord commended the unjust steward, forasmuch as he had done wisely: for the children of this world are wiser in their generation than the children of light.

9 And I say to you: Make unto you friends of the mammon of iniquity; that when you shall fail, they may receive you into everlasting dwellings.

canst be steward no longer. Our Lord, on the eve of His passion, promulgated this sentence upon earth: *Now shall the prince of this world be cast out.* By the apostolic preaching and by baptism, the devil was cast out from the hearts of a multitude, and the reign of paganism was broken.

The devil then *said within himself: What shall I do, because my lord taketh away from me the stewardship? To dig I am not able, to beg I am ashamed.* He is unable, that is, to accomplish any good work, and is ashamed to beg for mercy from his Creator. He therefore resolves on a new strategy to oppress mankind: by lessening the requirements of the Christian religion, he will deceive them under a guise of kindness, so that they will *receive* him rather than their Redeemer.

The devil tells mankind that they need not pay all the *oil* and *wheat* that they *owe.* Oil, in the Scriptures, is often a symbol of charity. He tells those who owe *an hundred barrels* that they need pay only *fifty,* persuading men that they can be saved if they keep only one of the two precepts of charity, either showing some kindness to their neighbour but not loving God with their whole heart, or else apparently loving God while neglecting their neighbour. Wheat, which springs up from the seed of the word, is a symbol for the true faith, which the devil wishes to corrupt. Here, he is more cautious, reducing a debt of *an hundred quarters* to *eighty.* If he sought to change much of the faith, it would be too obvious. But to falsify even one article of the creed suffices, since whoever obstinately disbelieves one revealed truth loses the virtue of faith, and thus, the hope of heaven.

The lord of the manor commends *the unjust steward* for acting *wisely,* not that God praises the devil, but because he had chosen a strategy well suited to its end and pursued it unswervingly. *The children of light* are rarely so single-minded in their doings. Yet all those with any power over temporal goods, will inevitably *make friends* by means of them: virtuous friends, if they use them virtuously, and evil friends, if they use them evilly. When their own life shall *fail,* they will find again friends whom they thus made on earth, glad to *receive* them *into* one of the two *everlasting dwellings.*

COMMENTARY ON ST. LUKE'S GOSPEL

10 He that is faithful in that which is least, is faithful also in that which is greater: and he that is unjust in that which is little, is unjust also in that which is greater.

11 If then you have not been faithful in the unjust mammon; who will trust you with that which is the true?

12 And if you have not been faithful in that which is another's; who will give you that which is your own?

13 No servant can serve two masters: for either he will hate the one and love the other; or he will hold to the one and despise the other. You cannot serve God and mammon.

14 Now the Pharisees, who were covetous, heard all these things: and they derided him.

15 And he said to them: You are they who justify yourselves before men, but God knoweth your hearts; for that which is high to men, is an abomination before God.

16 The law and the prophets were until John; from that time the kingdom of God is preached, and every one useth violence towards it.

17 And it is easier for heaven and earth to pass, than one tittle of the law to fall.

18 Every one that putteth away his wife, and marrieth another, committeth adultery: and he that marrieth her that is put away from her husband, commmitteth adultery.

vv. 10–18

Those who have been *faithful* to God in using temporal things, *which are least*, will then be entrusted *with that which is greater, the true* wealth of glory. Unlike the material possessions of this life, this wealth will be their *own*, since it will inhere in their soul and body.

Our Lord speaks of *mammon*, an Aramaic word for 'riches', as a person, in whose service one may be enrolled. According to the desert Fathers, experts in spiritual warfare, each of the capital sins has behind it some fallen angel, who has an affinity for that sin. Mammon seems therefore to denote the fallen angel whose province is avarice. No one can *love* such a being, but one might *hold to* him, even without knowing it, and *despise* God. By contrast, to love God implies that one will *hate* this demon.

When *derided* by the Pharisees, Christ speaks more mildly to them than at other times, lest He appear to be moved by anger; and so He simply tells them that *God knoweth* their *hearts*, not mentioning their *covetousness*. Later, He will use the same word, *abomination*, to refer to the *abomination of desolation*, which suggests that this will be something proving *high*, or impressive, *to men* under the sway of mammon.

The Pharisees could object that our Lord's warnings against mammon were contrary to Moses, who had promised earthly possessions as a reward for fidelity. He therefore tells them that that dispensation, given in the old *Law* and repeated by the *prophets* came to an end with *John* the Baptist, who had declared the Messias now present. It has been replaced by a higher *kingdom*, to enter which, men are obliged to do *violence* to fallen nature, restraining their desires for temporal things.

Lest this seem to belittle the teaching of Moses, the Lord indicates that the old law has an even higher dignity than they imagine: it will remain when *heaven and earth pass*, since every *tittle* of its symbols and prophecies will be forever fulfilled after the resurrection, in the true promised land. Yet there were things in that law which have now come to an end in their literal sense, of which the most necessary to be aware of is the toleration of divorce and re-marriage.

19 There was a certain rich man, who was clothed in purple and fine linen; and feasted sumptuously every day.

20 And there was a certain beggar, named Lazarus, who lay at his gate, full of sores,

21 Desiring to be filled with the crumbs that fell from the rich man's table, and no one did give him; moreover the dogs came and licked his sores.

22 And it came to pass, that the beggar died, and was carried by the angels into Abraham's bosom. And the rich man also died: and he was buried in hell.

23 And lifting up his eyes when he was in torments, he saw Abraham afar off, and Lazarus in his bosom:

24 And he cried, and said: Father Abraham, have mercy on me, and send Lazarus, that he may dip the tip of his finger in water, to cool my tongue: for I am tormented in this flame.

25 And Abraham said to him: Son, remember that thou didst receive good things in thy lifetime, and likewise Lazareth evil things, but now he is comforted; and thou art tormented.

26 And besides all this, between us and you, there is fixed a great chaos: so that they who would pass from hence to you, cannot, nor from thence come hither.

27 And he said: Then, father, I beseech thee, that thou wouldst send him to my father's house, for I have five brethren,

28 That he may testify unto them, lest they also come into this place of torments.

29 And Abraham said to him: They have Moses and the prophets; let them hear them.

30 But he said: No, father Abraham: but if one went to them from the dead, they will do penance.

31 And he said to him: If they hear not Moses and the prophets, neither will they believe, if one rise again from the dead.

think about it. If he has a sufficiently deep desire not to hear God's message, this is what he will do. By contrast, if a person desires the truth sufficiently to take the miracle seriously, he will already have accepted the teaching of the faith which he has heard from childhood. Hence, if the brothers have not believed *Moses and the prophets*, they would not believe the testimony of Lazarus back from the dead.

vv. 19–31

Having spoken somewhat obscurely, perhaps as a just punishment for their having derided him, He concludes with a clear teaching on the danger of avarice. Though it is often referred to as 'the parable of Dives (the rich man) and Lazarus', St Luke does not call it a parable; and there is no other place in the gospels where a proper name, such as Lazarus, is introduced into a parable. It may therefore be a simple description of two real people.[2]

Some have suggested that the rich man may be in *hell* in the wider sense of the word, more particularly in purgatory, rather than in hell in the sense of the place of lost souls. Yet this does not seem possible, since Abraham tells him that none may *from thence come hither*. The souls from purgatory would come to *Abraham's bosom*, that is, to the Limbo of the Fathers, when their expiation was over, there to await the coming of the Redeemer. Also, the rich man's *five brothers* will join him if they do not *do penance* nor *believe*, and one cannot reach purgatory if one has not penitence or faith.

One may wonder: why then does the rich man speak respectfully to Abraham, calling him *Father*, when it is believed that the damned blaspheme? During an exorcism, the demons are sometimes forced by the power of the Church's prayer to stop blaspheming and instead to give glory to God. Perhaps something similar is happening here.

Why does the rich man desire that his brothers not join him, when the damned are full of malice to others? Perhaps he desires this not out of love for them, but because he knows that he himself will be more mocked by the other souls, when they see his brothers come to join him; or else he fears the wrath of the brothers themselves. Or perhaps here also he is being forced to speak against his will, so that Abraham may instruct him.

Since even the greatest miracle does not make the object of faith itself visible, and since human minds are weak, it is always possible even for one who witnesses a miracle, such as someone risen *from the dead*, to persuade himself that there must be some natural explanation for what he has seen, or simply to refuse to

2 This is also suggested by the Church's liturgy for the dead, which prays that the departed soul may go to join Lazarus *quondam paupere,* "who once was poor".

1 And he said to his disciples: It is impossible that scandals should not come: but woe to him through whom they come.

2 It were better for him, that a millstone were hanged about his neck, and he cast into the sea, than that he should scandalize one of these little ones.

3 Take heed to yourselves. If thy brother sin against thee, reprove him: and if he do penance, forgive him.

4 And if he sin against thee seven times in a day, and seven times in a day be converted unto thee, saying, I repent; forgive him.

5 And the apostles said to the Lord: Increase our faith.

6 And the Lord said: If you had faith like to a grain of mustard seed, you might say to this mulberry tree, Be thou rooted up, and be thou transplanted into the sea: and it would obey you.

7 But which of you having a servant ploughing, or feeding cattle, will say to him, when he is come from the field: Immediately go, sit down to meat:

8 And will not rather say to him: Make ready my supper, and gird thyself, and serve me, whilst I eat and drink, and afterwards thou shalt eat and drink?

9 Doth he thank that servant, for doing the things which he commanded him?

10 I think not. So you also, when you shall have done all these things that are commanded you, say: We are unprofitable servants; we have done that which we ought to do.

vv. 1–4

TO CAUSE *SCANDALS* IS TO DO THINGS, whether or not they are wrong in themselves, that cause the weak to sin or stumble in their faith. The *little ones* are thus not necessarily children, but anyone whose weakness makes them easy to influence. Pharasaical scandal, by contrast, means that a person sins at the sight of another's actions not by weakness but by malice: thus the Pharisees in the gospels often turn further from the faith by maliciously judging Christ to be a law-breaker and too indulgent to sinners.

Since scandal is a sin against fraternal charity, Christ next enjoins a certain act of fraternal charity as a remedy against it: correction of the sinner. We are to *reprove* one who sins against us not because we have suffered some loss, but only out of love for his soul; and hence, only in such a way as we think likely to benefit him.

vv. 5–10

Do the apostles not yet have *faith like to a grain of mustard seed*? Earlier, our Lord has used this seed as an image for Himself, incarnate and obedient. The apostles will thus have a faith like a mustard seed, when they are transformed into His likeness and ready to suffer martyrdom. This readiness will enable them to *transplant* the *tree* of the Cross from Judea into the surging *sea* of the nations.

Yet so that they will not become proud, later on, when they see how they are converting the world, He tells them that evangelisation will not exhaust their duties. As well as serving God in their neighbour by *ploughing* up the consciences of the gentiles and *feeding* them with the word, they must also serve God in Himself: they must recollect or *gird* themselves in prayer, and perform the duties of the sacred liturgy, compared here to a *supper* because the Lord delights in it, and because He instituted its highest act after the Last Supper. *Afterwards*, in the next life, there will be time for the apostles to rest.

11 And it came to pass, as he was going to Jerusalem, he passed through the midst of Samaria and Galilee.

12 And as he entered into a certain town, there met him ten men that were lepers, who stood afar off;

13 And lifted up their voice, saying: Jesus, master, have mercy on us.

14 Whom when he saw, he said: Go, shew yourselves to the priests. And it came to pass, as they went, they were made clean.

15 And one of them, when he saw that he was made clean, went back, with a loud voice glorifying God.

16 And he fell on his face before his feet, giving thanks: and this was a Samaritan.

17 And Jesus answering, said, Were not ten made clean? and where are the nine?

18 There is no one found to return and give glory to God, but this stranger.

19 And he said to him: Arise, go thy way; for thy faith hath made thee whole.

Since gratitude is a virtue and Christ is not lacking in any virtue, why will the master not *thank that servant*? Fulfilling the duties of the active and contemplative life cannot strictly elicit gratitude, since gratitude acknowledges the giving of a gift rather than the accomplishment of a duty. But cannot we also do more than just the *things that are commanded* on pain of sin? Yes, but He does not speak of the fact that He will be grateful for this, since, as the philosopher says, the magnanimous man conceals his virtue.[1]

vv. 11–19

The Lord bids the lepers to show themselves *to the priests*, who, under the Law of Moses, had to judge if someone had been cured of leprosy. If a cure had occurred, the priest would take two sparrows: one sparrow would be sacrificed over running water, while the other would be bound to some wood, dipped in the blood of the first and then allowed to go free.[2] It is a mysterious image of the Redemption. The first sparrow symbolises Jesus, compared to a sparrow in the psalms; by its blood and the wood and the flowing water, the other bird is set free, symbolising us, washed in Christ's blood, united to the Cross by faith, and saved by the waters of baptism.

Nine of the lepers remain with the image and do not pass through to the reality. The *Samaritan*, who gives *glory to God*, though still a *stranger* until Pentecost, symbolises all who will arrive at the more perfect worship of the new covenant, and who will give thanks to the Father by prostrating themselves before the Son.

---

1 *Nicomachean Ethics* IV.3. Cf. St Thomas Aquinas, *Summa Theologiae*, 2a 2ae 129, 3: "The magnanimous man is said to employ irony, not insofar as this is contrary to truth, so as either to say of himself lowly things that are not true or to deny of himself great things that are true, but because he does not disclose all his greatness, especially to the large number of those who are beneath him."
2 See Leviticus, chapter 14.

20 And being asked by the Pharisees, when the kingdom of God should come? he answered them, and said: The kingdom of God cometh not with observation:

21 Neither shall they say: Behold here, or behold there. For lo, the kingdom of God is within you.

22 And he said to his disciples: The days will come, when you shall desire to see one day of the Son of man; and you shall not see it.

23 And they will say to you: See here, and see there. Go ye not after, nor follow them:

24 For as the lightening that lighteneth from under heaven, shineth unto the parts that are under heaven, so shall the Son of man be in his day.

25 But first he must suffer many things and be rejected by this generation.

26 And as it came to pass in the days of Noe, so shall it be also in the days of the Son of man.

27 They did eat and drink, they married wives, and were given in marriage, until the day that Noe entered into the ark: and the flood came and destroyed them all.

28 Likewise as it came to pass, in the days of Lot: they did eat and drink, they bought and sold, they planted and built.

29 And in the day that Lot went out of Sodom, it rained fire and brimstone from heaven, and destroyed them all.

30 Even thus shall it be in the day when the Son of man shall be revealed.

31 In that hour, he that shall be on the housetop, and his goods in the house, let him not go down to take them away: and he that shall be in the field, in like manner, let him not return back.

32 Remember Lot's wife.

33 Whosoever shall seek to save his life, shall lose it: and whosoever shall lose it, shall preserve it.

34 I say to you: in that night there shall be two men in one bed; the one shall be taken, and the other shall be left.

35 Two women shall be grinding together: the one shall be taken, and the other shall be left: two men shall be in the field; the one shall be taken, and the other shall be left.

36 They answering, say to him: Where, Lord?

37 Who said to them: Wheresoever the body shall be, thither will the eagles also be gathered together.

vv. 20–37

Although under the new covenant, God is to be glorified publicly by individuals and even by nations, this public worship must, to be acceptable, derive from supernatural life *within* the believer. The *kingdom of God* thus consists primarily in inward acts that are not directly subject to *observation*. Lest His disciples therefore wonder whether He would ever manifest Himself unmistakably to the world, He then speaks of the *day of the Son of man*. It is called *one* day, or more literally, 'one of the days', since not only will His final coming be seen by the whole world, it will also be foreshadowed by certain other dramatic triumphs of His Church in the course of history. We may think, for example, of the overthrow of Arianism and Iconoclasm, the coronation of Charlemagne, or the conversion of the Americas.

He warns the disciples against what today is sometimes called 'normality bias': the tendency of human beings to refuse to believe that something extraordinary is coming to pass, even when the evidence warrants such a belief. As *in the days of Noe* and *of Lot,* those who live in the last days will not attend to the prophetic warnings that God is about to punish the world for its sins, but will distract themselves by that which their own times have in common with all ages: food and *drink, marriage* with its preliminaries and consequences, trade, building, and agriculture. The preaching of Noe was met with incredulity, according to St Peter, and so we may suppose that this sin, as well as that of *Sodom*, will be prevalent in the last days.

The disciples apparently wish to know *where* the Lord will return, so that they may be able easily to find Him. But they do not need such details, since as part of the mystical *body* of Christ, and nourished, like *eagles*, by His sacramental *body*, they will already have been *gathered together* in His presence throughout their lives and therefore will be united to Him at His final coming.

CHAPTER 18

1 And he spoke also a parable to them, that we ought always to pray, and not to faint,

2 Saying: There was a judge in a certain city, who feared not God, nor regarded man.

3 And there was a certain widow in that city, and she came to him, saying: Avenge me of my adversary.

4 And he would not for a long time. But afterwards he said within himself: Although I fear not God, nor regard man,

5 Yet because this widow is troublesome to me, I will avenge her, lest continually coming she weary me.

6 And the Lord said: Hear what the unjust judge saith.

7 And will not God revenge his elect who cry to him day and night: and will he have patience in their regard?

8 I say to you, that he will quickly revenge them. But yet the Son of man, when he cometh, shall he find, think you, faith on earth?

9 And to some who trusted in themselves as just, and despised others, he spoke also this parable:

10 Two men went up into the temple to pray: the one a Pharisee, and the other a publican.

11 The Pharisee standing, prayed thus with himself: O God, I give thee thanks that I am not as the rest of men, extortioners, unjust, adulterers, as also is this publican.

12 I fast twice in a week: I give tithes of all that I possess.

13 And the publican, standing afar off, would not so much as lift up his eyes towards heaven; but struck his breast, saying: O god, be merciful to me a sinner.

14 I say to you, this man went down into his house justified rather that the other: because every one that exalteth himself, shall be humbled: and he that humbleth himself, shall be exalted.

THE PARABLE OF THE UNJUST JUDGE HAS at least two meanings. It may be read, first of all, as an exhortation to prayer. In this way, the argument proceeds 'from a contrary example': if even so ill-disposed a judge would be moved to do justice by the *continual coming* of a plaintiff, much more will God free *his elect who pray* to Him persistently.

Yet St Irenaeus, who learned his Christianity from the first disciples of the apostles, relates a second meaning. The unjust *judge in a certain city, who feared not God nor regarded man,* is antichrist: he is, in a way, already ruling in the city of man since, says St John, *even now there are become many Antichrists.* The *widow* who desires him to *avenge* her against her *adversary* will then no longer be the Church but rather the Synagogue: those Jews who do not believe in Christ and who wish to see an end to Christianity. Widowed of the old Law, they will *continually* desire a Messias who shall not be Jesus of Nazareth, thus calling unbeknownst to themselves for the coming of His rival. *After a long time,* this prayer will be heard.

Our Lord here predicts a decay of *faith* that will occur on earth, despite God's having so often *quickly* saved His people by the deaths of persecutors, and by sending great saints, doctors and miracle-workers. Therefore, lest anyone suppose that it will suffice to belong externally to this people without inward conversion, He adds a parable to show that the latter is necessary so that we may be *just* and acceptable in God's sight. The Pharisee is said to have *prayed with himself,* since he did not know the Father or the Son. Both he and the publican begin their prayer in a state of mortal sin, but the publican is enabled to make an act of perfect contrition, and so goes *down into his house justified.* Partly from this parable we draw the custom of striking the *breast,* a gesture which God has infused with a power to stir up compunction.

15 And they brought unto him also infants, that he might touch them. Which when the disciples saw, they rebuked them.

16 But Jesus, calling them together, said: Suffer children to come to me, and forbid them not: for of such is the kingdom of God.

17 Amen, I say to you: Whosoever shall not receive the kingdom of God as a child, shall not enter into it.

18 And a certain ruler asked him, saying: Good master, what shall I do to possess everlasting life?

19 And Jesus said to him: Why dost thou call me good? None is good but God alone.

20 Thou knowest the commandments: Thou shalt not kill: Thou shalt not commit adultery: Thou shalt not steal: Thou shalt not bear false witness: Honour thy father and mother.

21 Who said: All these things have I kept from my youth.

22 Which when Jesus had heard, he said to him: Yet one thing is wanting to thee: sell all whatever thou hast, and give to the poor, and thou shalt have treasure in heaven: and come, follow me.

23 He having heard these things, became sorrowful; for he was very rich.

24 And Jesus seeing him become sorrowful, said: How hardly shall they that have riches enter into the kingdom of God.

25 For it is easier for a camel to pass through the eye of a needle, than for a rich man to enter into the kingdom of God.

26 And they that heard it, said: Who then can be saved?

27 He said to them: The things that are impossible with men, are possible with God.

28 Then Peter said: Behold, we have left all things, and have followed thee.

29 Who said to them: Amen, I say to you, there is no man that hath left house, or parents, or brethren, or wife, or children, for the kingdom of God's sake,

30 Who shall not receive much more in this present time, and in the world to come life everlasting.

vv. 15–17

By saying *Suffer children to come to me*, Christ indicates that infants are to be baptised. Without baptism, they would remain in original sin, and therefore cut off from Him. While the natural simplicity of children is not itself a mark of holiness, no one can *enter the kingdom of God* unless he acquires a like simplicity by grace.

vv. 18–30

In His reply to the *young man*, our Lord does not deny that He is *good*, but on the contrary intimates His divinity. To have accepted the compliment without remark would have tended to confirm the young man in supposing that Jesus was good only as men are.

This young man will *possess everlasting life* in heaven if he continues to keep the commandments, but by selling what he has, he will also gain *treasure in heaven*, that is, a great increase in accidental beatitude: delight in contemplating the more abundant good works that he was enabled to do on earth, in virtue of having been freed from riches.

Any miracle in nature is *easier* than the justification of any soul, since by the former a creature is simply acted on by God, while by the latter a person participates in God's nature. Again, for *a camel to pass through the eye of a needle* would require only one divine intervention. For *a rich man to enter into the kingdom of God* normally requires many divine interventions, in the form of many sacraments and actual graces. Without these, it is *impossible* that a rich man be not induced sometimes by his wealth to break the law of God and so forfeit salvation.

How does a man *leave* his *wife for the kingdom of God's sake*? When the two of them part by mutual consent, to enter the religious life; or else when they remain together but practise perpetual continence.

31 Then Jesus took unto him the twelve, and said to them: Behold, we go up to Jerusalem, and all things shall be accomplished which were written by the prophets concerning the Son of man.

32 For he shall be delivered to the Gentiles, and shall be mocked, and scourged, and spit upon:

33 And after they have scourged him, they will put him to death; and the third day he shall rise again.

34 And they understood none of these things, and this word was hid from them, and they understood not the things that were said.

35 Now it came to pass, when he drew nigh to Jericho, that a certain blind man sat by the wayside, begging.

36 And when he heard the multitude passing by, he asked what this meant.

37 And they told him, that Jesus of Nazareth was passing by.

38 And he cried out, saying: Jesus, son of David, have mercy on me.

39 And they that went before, rebuked him, that he should hold his peace: but he cried out much more: Son of David, have mercy on me.

40 And Jesus standing, commanded him to be brought unto him. And when he was come near, he asked him,

41 Saying: What wilt thou that I do to thee? But he said: Lord, that I may see.

42 And Jesus said to him: Receive thy sight: thy faith hath made thee whole.

43 And immediately he saw, and followed him, glorifying God. And all the people, when they saw it, gave praise to God.

vv. 31–34

Since our Lord gives a clear prophecy of His passion, using no metaphor or parable, why do the apostles understand *none of these things*? They believe Him to be the Messias, and the Son of God, but they cannot yet grasp that He is sent to die for the sins of men: the charity of the Father and the Son is still *hid from them*. Jesus therefore opens the eyes of a blind man to suggest to them their own need of enlightenment.

vv. 35–43

Why do the men who first hear the blind beggar scold him, telling him to *hold his peace*? After all, it is natural to feel sympathy for someone in such a plight, rather than to deny him the chance of a cure. It is because of the title, *Son of David*, which he gives to Christ. This was not like saying 'Rabbi' or 'Master': it meant 'Messias', and as such it was a dangerous title, liable to give serious annoyance to Herod and Pontius Pilate. The beggar realises that he is causing a stir, and so to draw even more attention to himself, he now drops the name *Jesus,* and uses only the messianic title, even doing so *much more*.

Christ does not go towards him, perhaps because being blind, the beggar would not have seen Him approach. He orders *him to be brought to* Himself, so that the blind man in his excited state may have some moments to grow calm. Since it is now so near to His death, our Lord no longer refuses a public profession of *faith* that He is indeed the Son of David, the Messias. If it is from a blind beggar that He first accepts it, this is both from humility and to suggest the state of the human race in need of its Saviour.

1 And entering in, he walked through Jericho.

2 And behold, there was a man named Zacheus, who was the chief of the publicans, and he was rich.

3 And he sought to see Jesus who he was, and he could not for the crowd, because he was low of stature.

4 And running before, he climbed up into a sycamore tree, that he might see him; for he was to pass that way.

5 And when Jesus was come to the place, looking up, he saw him, and said to him: Zacheus, make haste and come down; for this day I must abide in thy house.

6 And he made haste and came down; and received him with joy.

7 And when all saw it, they murmured, saying that he was gone to be a guest with a man that was a sinner.

8 But Zacheus standing, said to the Lord: Behold, Lord, the half of my goods I give to the poor; and if I have wronged any man of any thing, I restore him fourfold.

9 Jesus said to him: This day is salvation come to this house, because he also is a son of Abraham.

10 For the Son of man is come to seek and to save that which was lost.

11 As they were hearing these things, he added and spoke a parable, because he was nigh to Jerusalem, and because they thought that the kingdom of God should immediately be manifested.

12 He said therefore: A certain nobleman went into a far country, to receive for himself a kingdom, and to return.

13 And calling his ten servants, he gave them ten pounds, and said to them: Trade till I come.

14 But his citizens hated him: and they sent an embassage after him, saying: We will not have this man to reign over us.

15 And it came to pass, that he returned, having received the kingdom: and he commanded his servants to be called, to whom he had given the money, that he might

COMMENTARY

VV. 1–10

ADAM, IN THE PARABLE OF THE GOOD
Samaritan, *went down from Jerusalem to Jericho.* The new
Adam, about to undo the effects of the Fall, makes
His final public journey in reverse, from Jericho to Jerusalem.

Zacheus must go to the trouble of climbing a tree: "no one
sees Jesus easily", notes St Ambrose.

He gives only *half of* his *goods to the poor,* since had he given
them all away, he would have been unable to *restore fourfold* what
he had wrongly taken.

Why does our Lord speak of Zacheus as a *son of Abraham,* rather
than as a son of Jacob or of Isaac? He gives him the name of
greatest dignity, the better to cure the murmuring of the crowd;
also because Abraham too had been *rich,* and yet detached from
his wealth.

VV. 11–27

He tells the next parable to show that there will be an interval
between His receiving the *kingdom* and this kingdom's being
manifested.[1] As the Son of David, He is Himself the *nobleman,*
who *went into a far country,* into heaven itself, there *to receive for
himself a kingdom* from His Father, *who hath subjected all things under
his feet,* until the time comes for Him *to return,* on the last day.

On Easter Sunday, in the evening, He called *ten servants,* the
ten apostles, to each of whom He gave a *pound,* bestowing on
all alike the right to forgive sins, and bidding them and their
successors *trade* till His *return,* that is, to increase His possessions by expending this sacramental power.

1   It is inept to call it "Luke's version of the parable of the talents". The parable of the talents, in chapter 25 of St Matthew, is a different one altogether.

know how much every man had gained by trading.

16 And the first came, saying: Lord, thy pound hath gained ten pounds.

17 And he said to him: Well done, thou good servant, because thou hast been faithful in a little, thou shalt have power over ten cities.

18 And the second came, saying: Lord, thy pound hath gained five pounds.

19 And he said to him: Be thou also over five cities.

20 And another came, saying: Lord, behold here is thy pound, which I have kept laid up in a napkin;

21 For I feared thee, because thou art an austere man: thou takest up what thou didst not lay down, and thou reapest that which thou didst not sow.

22 He saith to him: Out of thy own mouth I judge thee, thou wicked servant. Thou knewest that I was an austere man, taking up what I laid not down, and reaping that which I did not sow:

23 And why then didst thou not give my money into the bank, that at my coming, I might have exacted it with usury?

24 And he said to them that stood by: Take the pound away from him, and give it to him that hath ten pounds.

25 And they said to him: Lord, he hath ten pounds.

26 But I say to you, that to every one that hath shall be given, and he shall abound: and from him that hath not, even that which he hath, shall be taken from him.

27 But as for those my enemies, who would not have me reign over them, bring them hither, and kill them before me.

Men become *citizens* of His kingdom by baptism. But these citizens have sometimes *hated* their king, not wishing to subject their private and public lives to His sway. And as often as baptised people have agreed to choose representatives who would refuse His kingship, by making society to be secular, that is, unchristian, so often have *his citizens sent an embassage after him, saying:We will not have this man to reign over us.*

Yet He returns *having received his kingdom*, since *the Son of man shall come in his majesty*, and His servants the clergy will be manifested to all as faithful or unfaithful, and be honoured in proportion to their zeal. Since a *napkin* or face-cloth is used either in eating or to wipe away sweat, the one who *laid up* his *pound* in the napkin seems to be the cleric who concealed the silver of God's word for the sake of his own comfort.

The king does not disavow the description of Himself as *taking up what* He *laid not down* and *reaping that which* He *did not sow*, since He puts to good use even skills that a person acquires without divine grace, and truths that a person learns from those who did not represent Him, once that person has come to faith. For Christ is *an austere man*, that is, strict in upholding the rights of His Father's kingdom, to which no skill or truth can be alien. All the more, therefore, ought the *wicked servant* to have laboured to increase that kingdom. Even a cleric who does not do this by extraordinary labours among unbelievers, may do so at least by putting the *money into the bank*, that is, by faithfully preaching the word of God in the Church, as in a safe and well-guarded house. Such preaching cannot fail to bear fruit, and so Christ would have received the *usury*, that is, the increase, in the number and merit of the faithful on His return.

Why does He make *usury*, a wicked activity, into an image of something good, namely, preaching? Usury is wrong because it treats something dead, money, as if it were alive and fruitful. The *word of God*, by contrast, *is living and effectual*, and divine grace increases when communicated to another. The idle servant, however, treats something living as if it were inert, and so his sin is, in the spiritual realm, the mirror-image of the usurer's sin in the material one.

28 And having said these things, he went before, going up to Jerusalem.

29 And it came to pass, when he was come nigh to Bethphage and Bethania, unto the mount called Olivet, he sent two of his disciples,

30 Saying: Go into the town which is over against you, at your entering into which you shall find the colt of an ass tied, on which no man ever hath sitten: loose him, and bring him hither.

31 And if any man shall ask you: Why do you loose him? you shall say thus unto him:

Because the Lord hath need of his service.

32 And they that were sent, went their way, and found the colt standing, as he had said unto them.

33 And as they were loosing the colt, the owners thereof said to them: Why loose you the colt?

34 But they said: Because the Lord hath need of him.

35 And they brought him to Jesus. And casting their garments on the colt, they set Jesus thereon.

36 And as he went, they spread their clothes underneath in the way.

The infidelity of one of Christ's ministers redounds to the greater glory of another, either because at the last judgement, the latter's fidelity appears more clearly by contrast, or because he benefits the souls that the former neglected, and so the unused *pound* is given *to him that hath the ten pounds*, while the angels who *stood by* marvel at the mysterious ways of divine providence.

Toward the end of the parable, our Lord places in the mouth of the king a saying that the disciples have already heard Him speak in His own person, concerning the exaltation of *the humble*. In this way He makes it even clearer that He is the one who is to travel to a far country to receive kingly power, and also that the time is drawing near when the minds of the disciples will be enlightened to understand the Scriptures.

Those laity who actively tried to obstruct the reign of Christ on earth will also be brought before Him at His return. His ministers are to *kill them* in His presence, that is, announce the divine sentence that will cut them off for ever from any possibility of sharing in the divine life.

vv. 28–36

Although Christ's kingdom is spiritual, distinct from the temporal kingdoms of earth, He nevertheless has jurisdiction over temporal things also, since *the earth is the Lord's and the fullness thereof.* He could therefore make use of a *colt* that had other *owners.* We may presume that these owners were enlightened to accept the reply of the *two disciples*. Since this temporary appropriation of the colt was an exercise of His kingly power, the animal itself was fittingly used for the manifestation of this kingship, in His public entry into Jerusalem on Palm Sunday.

37 And when he was now coming near the descent of mount Olivet, the whole multitude of his disciples began with joy to praise God with a loud voice, for all the mighty works they had seen,

38 Saying: Blessed be the king who cometh in the name of the Lord, peace in heaven, and glory on high!

39 And some of the Pharisees, from amongst the multitude, said to him: Master, rebuke thy disciples.

40 To whom he said: I say to you, that if these shall hold their peace, the stones will cry out.

41 And when he drew near, seeing the city, he wept over it, saying:

42 If thou also hadst known, and that in this thy day, the things that are to thy peace; but now they are hidden from thy eyes.

43 For the days shall come upon thee, and thy enemies shall cast a trench about thee, and compass thee round, and straiten thee on every side,

44 And beat thee flat to the ground, and thy children who are in thee: and they shall not leave in thee a stone upon a stone: because thou hast not known the time of thy visitation.

45 And entering into the temple, he began to cast out them that sold therein, and them that bought.

46 Saying to them: It is written: My house is the house of prayer. But you have made it a den of thieves.

47 And he was teaching daily in the temple. And the chief priests and the scribes and the rulers of the people sought to destroy him:

48 And they found not what to do to him: for all the people were very attentive to hear him.

v. 37

At His birth, the angels declare peace on earth; now, before His death, men declare *peace in heaven*.

vv. 38–44

On Good Friday, when the crowd were induced by fear to *hold their peace*, *the stones* would as it were *cry out*, since *the rocks were rent* at Christ's death. Later still, when the Jewish authorities sought to smother the spread of the gospel among their fellow country-men, it spread to the gentiles, who were changed from being like stones in regard to the word of God, to crying out in praise of God's deeds.

Our Lord never *wept* over Jerusalem when He was disputing with the rulers or being threatened with death, but only on the day of His triumphant entry, showing that He did not grieve over it from disappointment or chagrin.

vv. 45–48

Those who *bought* and *sold* in the temple are *thieves* not only of money, but of the honour due the house of God.

1 And it came to pass, that on one of the days, as he was teaching the people in the temple, and preaching the gospel, the chief priests and the scribes, with the ancients, met together,

2 And spoke to him, saying: Tell us, by what authority dost thou these things? or, Who is he that hath given thee this authority?

3 And Jesus answering, said to them: I will also ask you one thing. Answer me:

4 The baptism of John, was it from heaven, or of men?

5 But they thought within themselves, saying: If we shall say, From heaven: he will say: Why then did you not believe him?

6 But if we say, Of men, the whole people will stone us: for they are persuaded that John was a prophet.

7 And they answered, that they knew not whence it was.

8 And Jesus said to them: Neither do I tell thee by what authority I do these things.

9 And he began to speak to the people this parable: A certain man planted a vineyard, and let it out to husbandmen: and he was abroad for a long time.

10 And at the season he sent a servant to the husbandmen, that they should give him of the fruit of the vineyard. Who, beating him, sent him away empty.

11 And again he sent another servant. But they beat him also, and treating him reproachfully, sent him away empty.

vv. 1–8

THE *CHIEF PRIESTS* FORM THE RELIGIOUS hierarchy, with the *scribes* as their chosen theologians, while the *ancients* are the most influential laity among the Jews. These three groups compose the Sanhedrin, with its seventy members.

In itself, the question that they pose to the Lord is a reasonable one, as the Sanhedrin has the duty of ensuring that impostors do not seduce the people. In reply, He might have spoken of His miracles as an adequate sign of His mission, but instead, from humility and to honour the precursor, He mentions *John*, who had given testimony of Him. The Jewish rulers *did not believe* John: they made no public statement about his mission, and did not intervene when Herod imprisoned him unjustly and then executed him. Herod remained a Jew in good standing, and was in Jerusalem at this very Passover. Since the Jewish rulers had thus allowed the rule of law to break down, they had the less right now to try to enforce the law; and since they had shown that they did not want to accept the testimony that John had given about Jesus, even though this testimony was accredited by the holiness of John's life and death, they had no right to demand some alternative proof of the Lord's *authority*. Hence, both in justice, to rebuke their guilt, and in mercy, lest they reject another proof of His right to preach, He will not tell them what they ask.

vv. 9–18

The *vineyard* is the privilege of being God's people, and its *fruit* are the works of faith, hope and love. The *husbandmen* are false prophets, and unjust priests and temporal rulers, while the three servants sent to gather this fruit are the smaller number of true prophets, and just priests and temporal rulers raised up during Israel's history from the time of Moses onward. The authorities in our Lord's time did not admit His divinity, but since they culpably deceived themselves into not recognising

COMMENTARY ON ST. LUKE'S GOSPEL

12 And again he sent the third: and they wounded him also, and cast him out.

13 Then the lord of the vineyard said: What shall I do? I will send my beloved son: it may be, when they see him, they will reverence him.

14 Whom when the husbandmen saw, they thought within themselves, saying: This is the heir, let us kill him, that the inheritance may be ours.

15 So casting him out of the vineyard, they killed him. What therefore will the lord of the vineyard do to them?

16 He will come, and will destroy these husbandmen, and will give the vineyard to others. Which they hearing, said to him: God forbid.

17 But he looking on them, said: What is this then that is written, The stone, which the builders rejected, the same is become the head of the corner?

18 Whosoever shall fall upon that stone, shall be bruised: and upon whomsoever it shall fall, it will grind him to powder.

19 And the chief priests and the scribes sought to lay hands on him the same hour: but they feared the people, for they knew that he spoke this parable to them.

20 And being upon the watch, they sent spies, who should feign themselves just, that they might take hold of him in his words, that they might deliver him up to the authority and power of the governor.

21 And they asked him, saying: Master, we know that thou speakest and teachest rightly: and thou dost not respect any person, but teachest the way of God in truth.

22 Is it lawful for us to give tribute to Caesar, or no?

23 But he considering their guile, said to them: Why tempt you me?

24 Shew me a penny. Whose image and inscription hath it? They answering, said to him, Caesar's.

25 And he said to them: Render therefore to Caesar the things that are Caesar's: and to God the things that are God's.

26 And they could not reprehend his word before the people: and wondering at his answer, they held their peace.

it, and in this way chose *to detain the truth of God in injustice*, they are said to have *thought within themselves: This is the heir.*

Since these *builders* do not want Christ, the *stone*, He becomes the *head* of a new building, the Catholic Church, to whom God *will give the vineyard.* The Jews who *fall upon that stone* by treating Christ as a false prophet *shall be bruised*, suffering much, and yet they shall not die, since Israel will remain; when the Church shall fall upon the nations, however, *it will grind* them *to powder*, leaving nothing of their ancient paganism behind.[1]

vv. 19–26

The *spies* wish either to weaken His popularity by making Him appear a supporter of Roman rule, or else to make Him guilty of sedition. He asks them to *shew* Him *a penny*, since He has none. He speaks as if He, unlike them, did not recognise the emperor's *image and inscription*, lest He seem to be subject by right to *Caesar's* authority, as opposed to freely subjecting Himself to Caesar's power.

If they must *render* the coin to Caesar because, having his name and inscription, it belongs to him, does this mean that we must give all our money to the government? It belongs to a government to establish a currency, and in this sense, money is its possession. Taxation is a legitimate charge made by the temporal power for the use of the currency that it alone may originate and, in this sense, owns. It is thus that money must be given to Caesar because it belongs to him.

---

1 Our Lord is apparently referring here to Dan 2:31–35, when the stone cut without hands from the mountain (an image for the virgin birth) strikes the statue of different metals (representing the succession of pagan empires), so that the metals are broken to tiny pieces and are blown away like chaff.

27 And there came to him some of the Sadducees, who deny that there is any resurrection, and they asked him,

28 Saying: Master, Moses wrote unto us, If any man's brother die, having a wife, and he leave no children, that his brother should take her to wife, and raise up seed unto his brother.

29 There were therefore seven brethren: and the first took a wife and died without children.

30 And the next took her to wife, and he also died childless.

31 And the third took her. And in like manner all the seven, and they left no children, and died.

32 Last of all the woman died also.

33 In the resurrection therefore, whose wife of them shall she be? For all the seven had her to wife.

34 And Jesus said to them: The children of this world marry, and are given in marriage:

35 But they that shall be accounted worthy of that world, and of the resurrection from the dead, shall neither be married, nor take wives.

36 Neither can they die any more: for they are equal to the angels, and are the children of God, being the children of the resurrection.

37 Now that the dead rise again, Moses also shewed, at the bush, when he called the Lord, The God of Abraham, and the God of Isaac, and the God of Jacob;

38 For he is not the God of the dead, but of the living: for all live to him.

Christ therefore escapes the trap by distinguishing this temporal power of the Romans from the spiritual power possessed by those whose principal task is to further *the things that are God's*, namely, religious worship and the life of faith. To pay taxes does not imply lessening the rights of the latter power. Yet did the Romans have the right to exercise even temporal power in the Holy Land, since this territory had been given by God to the Jews? Strictly speaking, they had not this right, and yet the Jews had the duty to obey, at least insofar as there was no possibility of maintaining a successful resistance to it.

vv. 27–40

The *Sadducees* do not put their question in good faith, but in order to mock the idea of a *resurrection*, in which they do not believe. His reply intimates a warning that for them there may indeed be no glorious resurrection, which is only for those *accounted worthy of that* future *world*. It is because no one will *die* in that world that there will be no more *marriage*. This shows that the primary purpose of marriage is to raise up offspring to replace the dead. For the *children of the resurrection* possess the beatific vision, which both gives their souls a beatitude *equal to the angels*, and their bodies perpetual vigour.

Since God is boundless life, it is impossible that He identify Himself by reference to persons who have no life, since such a name or title would convey a false idea of Himself. Hence, *Abraham, Isaac*, and *Jacob* are all living. But since they are no longer living in their bodies, they must be living in their souls, in a way that is knowable *to him*, that is, to God. Therefore, the soul is immortal. But the soul will not be allowed to remain for ever without its body, since the two naturally belong together. Therefore, *the dead rise again*.

39 And some of the scribes answering, said to him: Master, thou hast said well.

40 And after that they durst not ask him any more questions.

41 But he said to them: How say they that Christ is the son of David?

42 And David himself saith in the book of Psalms: The Lord said to my Lord, sit thou on my right hand,

43 Till I make thy enemies thy footstool.

44 David then calleth him Lord: and how is he his son?

45 And in the hearing of all the people, he said to his disciples:

46 Beware of the scribes, who desire to walk in long robes, and love salutations in the marketplace, and the first chairs in the synagogues, and the chief rooms at feasts:

47 Who devour the houses of widows, feigning long prayer. These shall receive greater damnation.

vv. 41–47

The *scribes* are glad to see the Sadducees discomforted. But lest He seem to weaken the authority of His teaching by accepting the support of these scribes, whose interpretations of the Scripture are false, He immediately discomforts them by asking them what the hundred and ninth psalm teaches about the Messias. The riddle can be solved only by recognising that the Messias will be both God and man, the *son of David* according to the flesh and *Lord* by His divinity.

Finally, since the scribes have come to *feign themselves just* and *deliver him up to the power of the governor* for crimes, such as sedition, which He has not committed, He openly reproves them for crimes that they have committed against *widows*, and reveals their lack of justice, shown by their desire for human honour. While it is fitting to give some outward token of respect to those with some distinctive religious function or state, it is a sin for such people to desire these tokens as if they were intended to terminate in themselves and not to pass on to God whom they represent.

Why does Christ unveil the scribes' hidden sins of ambition *in the hearing of all the people*, given that it is not yet time for the secrets of all hearts to be made known? Perhaps because the scribes are accustomed to veil sins that they commit against third parties, when they devour *the houses of widows*. Since they do this by *feigning long prayer*, and thus making religion hateful, they will receive a greater *damnation*, if they do not repent, than will common thieves.

1 And looking on, he saw the rich men cast their gifts into the treasury.

2 And he saw also a certain poor widow casting in two brass mites.

3 And he said: Verily I say to you, that this poor widow hath cast in more than they all:

4 For all these have of their abundance cast into the offerings of God: but she of her want, hath cast in all the living that she had.

5 And some saying of the temple, that it was adorned with goodly stones and gifts, he said:

6 These things which you see, the days will come in which there shall not be left a stone upon a stone that shall not be thrown down.

7 And they asked him, saying: Master, when shall these things be? and what shall be the sign when they shall begin to come to pass?

8 Who said: Take heed you be not seduced; for many will come in my name, saying, I am he; and the time is at hand: go ye not therefore after them.

9 And when you shall hear of wars and seditions, be not terrified: these things must first come to pass; but the end is not yet presently.

10 Then he said to them: Nation shall rise against nation, and kingdom against kingdom.

11 And there shall be great earthquakes in diverse places, and pestilences, and famines, and terrors from heaven; and there shall be great signs.

12 But before all these things, they will lay their hands upon you, and persecute you, delivering you up to the synagogues and into prisons, dragging you before kings and governors, for my name's sake.

13 And it shall happen unto you for a testimony.

14 Lay it up therefore into your hearts, not to meditate before how you shall answer:

15 For I will give you a mouth and wisdom, which all your adversaries shall not be able to resist and gainsay.

16 And you shall be betrayed by your parents and brethren, and kinsmen and friends;

VV. 1–24

ST LUKE DOES NOT RECORD THE OTHER half of the question that the apostles put to Christ, about the time of His return and the end of the world, perhaps to direct his readers' attention more toward the imminent fall of Jerusalem. However, we know from St Matthew that Christ's words are an answer to both parts of the question.

Why did our Lord not more explicitly correct the apparent assumption of the apostles that the destruction of the temple would usher in or accompany the end of the world? Perhaps in part because it would have meant teaching them explicitly about the *diminution* of the Jews mentioned by St Paul, and the entering in of the Gentiles; this may have been one of the things which, as He said at the Last Supper, they were not yet ready to hear. However, this teaching is implied when He speaks of *the times of the nations.*

Again, the apostles were in a way correct in joining the destruction of the temple and the end of the world. The former was a figure of the latter. The destruction of the temple brought the old covenant to a close, while Christ's coming in glory will put an end to the forms of worship that He instituted for the new covenant: the Mass or divine liturgy will no longer be offered, nor any sacraments administered. For although the new covenant is everlasting, its ceremonies are not, and so He can say that not only earth, the old covenant, but also *heaven will pass away.*

Although the first half of the discourse can therefore be understood of the events preceding the end of the world, it seems primarily to refer to the fall of Jerusalem, until and including the prophecy that the Jews would be *led away captives into all nations.*

Terrors from heaven were seen in the city before the destruction of the temple in AD 70. Josephus, a historian contemporary with these events, records that "there was a star resembling a

and some of you they will put to death.

17 And you shall be hated by all men for my name's sake.

18 But a hair of your head shall not perish.

19 In your patience you shall possess your souls.

20 And when you shall see Jerusalem compassed about with an army; then know that the desolation thereof is at hand.

21 Then let those who are in Judea, flee to the mountains; and those who are in the midst thereof, depart out:

and those who are in the countries, not enter into it.

22 For these are the days of vengeance, that all things may be fulfilled, that are written.

23 But woe to them that are with child and give suck in those days; for there shall be great distress in the land, and wrath upon this people.

24 And they shall fall by the edge of the sword; and shall be led away captives into all nations; and Jerusalem shall be trodden down by the Gentiles; till the times of the nations be fulfilled.

25 And there shall be signs in the sun, and in the moon, and in the stars; and upon the earth distress of nations, by reason of the confusion of the roaring of the sea and of the waves;

26 Men withering away for fear, and expectation of what shall come upon the whole world. For the powers of heaven shall be moved;

27 And then they shall see the Son of man coming in

a cloud, with great power and majesty.

28 But when these things begin to come to pass, look up, and lift up your heads, because your redemption is at hand.

29 And he spoke to them in a similitude. See the fig tree, and all the trees:

30 When they now shoot forth their fruit, you know that summer is nigh;

sword, which stood over the city, and a comet, that continued a whole year".[1]

After the Jews have been led away from Jerusalem, which happened both after the destruction of the temple, and at the end of their second and final revolt in AD 135, it will be *trodden down by the nations*, that is, by people not descended from Jacob. To tread down does not imply misusing power, but exercising it, since Christ gave the seventy-two a power to tread down *serpents and scorpions*, or evil spirits, as we read in chapter ten. Hence the *times of the nations* include the period during which Jerusalem was governed by Catholics, that is, from the fourth century to the seventh, and again during the twelfth. Yet the phrase 'tread down' also suggests something of violence, perhaps because it is unnatural when the Jews are excluded from the governance of the city acquired for them by King David.

In speaking of the *times* rather than the *time* of the nations, Christ may be indicating the succession of powers to which the city will be subject: pagan and imperial, Catholic and imperial, Arab Muslim, Turkish Muslim, Crusader, Turkish once again. These times appear to have now been *fulfilled*, given that the Jews took possession once again of the city in 1967. This event, accordingly, was preceded by the apostasy of once Catholic nations, which no longer publicly recognise Him or His Church.

vv. 25–38

The last part of the discourse, from *there shall be signs in the sun* seems to refer primarily to the period immediately preceding the second coming. Although *men*, that is, those who seek a merely human happiness, will be in *distress* and *fear* at these signs, the disciples of Christ are to *lift up* their *heads*, and be glad that the world as they know it is ending.

In St Matthew's and St Mark's gospel, our Lord says to the four apostles: *From the fig tree, learn a parable. When the branch thereof is now tender, and the leaves come forth, you know that summer is nigh.* Here, He says something different: *See the fig tree and all the trees: when they now shoot forth their fruit, you know that summer*

1 *On the Jewish War,* Book VI: 5.

31 So you also, when you shall see these things come to pass, know that the kingdom of God is at hand.

32 Amen, I say to you, this generation shall not pass away, till all things be fulfilled.

33 Heaven and earth shall pass away, but my words shall not pass away.

34 And take heed to yourselves, lest perhaps your hearts be overcharged with surfeiting and drunkenness, and the cares of this life, and that day come upon you suddenly.

35 For as a snare shall it come upon all that sit upon the face of the whole earth.

36 Watch ye, therefore, praying at all times, that you may be accounted worthy to escape all these things that are to come, and to stand before the Son of man.

37 And in the daytime, he was teaching in the temple; but at night, going out, he abode in the mount that is called Olivet.

38 And all the people came early in the morning to him in the temple, to hear him.

is nigh. Moreover, St Luke separates this saying from what precedes it, whereas St Matthew and St Mark relate an unbroken discourse. We may therefore conclude that our Lord spoke this saying recorded by St Luke at a different moment, perhaps in repeating the discourse, or a part of it, for a larger group of disciples. What is the significance of this?

The *fig-tree* is an image for the Jewish people. In St Matthew and St Mark, Christ curses the fig-tree that produces only leaves and not fruit, to show that this people, insofar as it was represented by its spiritual and temporal rulers, professed obedience to God but did not bring forth the fruit of faith, hope and charity, and so put their Messias to death. When therefore these two evangelists record Him as saying of the fig-tree just afterward: *When the branch thereof is now tender, and the leaves come forth, you know that summer is nigh*; *so you also, when you shall see all these things, know that it is nigh, at the doors,* we may understand Him to mean that when the rulers of His people offer lip-service only, persecution is about to blaze upon them.

St Luke, however, speaks not of leaves but of fruit, and not only of the fig-tree but also of all the trees. If the fig-tree represents the Jews, it is reasonable to see *all the* other *trees* as referring to all the other nations. When all of them together bear fruit, this is a sign that *the kingdom of God*, and the second coming, *is at hand.*

This generation, that is, those living at the time, *did not* all *pass away* until Jerusalem had been besieged and its temple destroyed. But 'generation' in Scripture has also the wider meaning of 'those who belong to a given class', as when the psalmist, having described the qualities of the just, says: *This is the generation of them that seek the face of the God of Jacob.* Hence, the class that consists of the disciples of Christ, that is, the Church, will continue until all the prophecies of the discourse are *fulfilled.*

Christ's warning against *surfeiting and drunkenness* again suggests that this part of His words were spoken to a larger group, and not just to the four principal apostles.

1 Now the feast of unleavened bread, which is called the pasch, was at hand.

2 And the chief priests and the scribes sought how they might put Jesus to death: but they feared the people.

3 And Satan entered into Judas, who was surnamed Iscariot, one of the twelve.

4 And he went, and discoursed with the chief priests and the magistrates, how he might betray him to them.

5 And they were glad, and covenanted to give him money.

6 And he promised. And he sought opportunity to betray him in the absence of the multitude.

7 And the day of the unleavened bread came, on which it was necessary that the pasch should be killed.

8 And he sent Peter and John, saying: Go, and prepare for us the pasch, that we may eat.

9 But they said: Where wilt thou that we prepare?

10 And he said to them: Behold, as you go into the city, there shall meet you a man carrying a pitcher of water: follow him into the house where he entereth in.

11 And you shall say to the goodman of the house: The master saith to thee, Where is the guest chamber, where I may eat the pasch with my disciples?

12 And he will shew you a large dining room, furnished; and there prepare.

13 And they going, found as he had said to them, and made ready the pasch.

14 And when the hour was come, he sat down, and the twelve apostles with him.

15 And he said to them: With desire I have desired to eat this pasch with you, before I suffer.

16 For I say to you, that from this time I will not eat it, till it be fulfilled in the kingdom of God.

17 And having taken the chalice, he gave thanks, and said: Take, and divide it among you:

18 For I say to you, that I will not drink of the fruit of the vine, till the kingdom of God come.

vv. 1–13

WHY DOES OUR LORD GIVE ST PETER AND St John a prophetic sign to bring them to the *house* for the pasch, rather than simply telling them where to go? Perhaps the greatness of the miracle that He was to work there made it fitting that they first receive this new token of His divinity. Perhaps also because the house foreshadows the Church, and He wished to show that the Church cannot be recognised for what it is by human intelligence alone. Why is the sign to *follow a man carrying a pitcher of water*? We enter the house of the Church by water and by a man, that is, by baptism.

vv. 14–18

He *desired with desire to eat this pasch*, or passover lamb, since it is here that He institutes the Holy Eucharist as the sacrifice of the new covenant, as the food of the disciples, and as the means by which He would remain on earth close to His friends until His second coming.

He would *not eat* the pasch again *until it* was *fulfilled in the kingdom of God*; and so, after the passover lamb was finished, He fulfils the kingdom by instituting and eating its greatest sacrament,

19 And taking bread, he gave thanks, and brake; and gave to them, saying: This is my body, which is given for you. Do this for a commemoration of me.

20 In like manner the chalice also, after he had supped, saying: This is the chalice, the new testament in my blood, which shall be shed for you.

21 But yet behold, the hand of him that betrayeth me is with me on the table.

22 And the Son of man indeed goeth, according to that which is determined: but yet, woe to that man by whom he shall be betrayed.

23 And they began to inquire among themselves, which of them it was that should do this thing.

24 And there was also a strife amongst them, which of them should seem to be the greater.

25 And he said to them: The kings of the Gentiles lord it over them; and they that have power over them, are called beneficent.

26 But you not so: but he that is the greater among you, let him become as the younger; and he that is the leader, as he that serveth.

27 For which is greater, he that sitteth at table, or he that serveth? Is it not he that sitteth at table? But I am in the midst of you, as he that serveth:

foreshadowed by the Jewish pasch. He also eats it again at every Mass insofar as the faithful, the members of His body, eat it.

The first chalice mentioned is a part of the passover meal, not the Eucharistic chalice. Just as the passover lamb is symbolic of what He will eat when the new covenant is instituted, which is already a first coming of *the kingdom of God*, so the wine is symbolic of what He will then *drink*. Likewise, the Holy Eucharist itself is symbolic of the communion that He will give to His friends when the *kingdom of God* will have fully *come*, at the resurrection of the just.

vv. 19–23

He takes *bread*, not at the Last Supper, but once this meal has been eaten; the new pasch does not begin, as He has twice said, till the old one is over.

In telling the apostles to *do* what He has done, He ordains them as priests of the new covenant, giving them the power to convert bread and wine into His body and blood, as a sacrifice that is also the *commemoration* of His death. Hence, His *blood shall be shed* for them; but more literally, the Greek word used by St Luke declares that this blood *is being* shed for them, since Jesus is already offering His sacrifice by anticipation, as the apostles will offer it in commemoration.

vv. 24–27

At so solemn a moment, how can the apostles contend about *which of them should seem to be the greater*? St Bede remarks that while the cause is unknown, it may have been a holy *strife*, in which each sought to give precedence to another. Or it may be that the apostles were struck to see Christ give a special honour to Judas, as St John tells us, and wondered whether Judas occupied a higher place among them than they had supposed.

What is wrong with *the kings of the Gentiles* being *called beneficent*? Such praise suggests that their realms are their own possessions, and that the services they render to their subjects are supererogatory, like the alms-giving of a benefactor, rather than acts to be done from justice.

28 And you are they who have continued with me in my temptations:

29 And I dispose to you, as my Father hath disposed to me, a kingdom;

30 That you may eat and drink at my table, in my kingdom: and may sit upon thrones, judging the twelve tribes of Israel.

31 And the Lord said: Simon, Simon, behold Satan hath desired to have you, that he may sift you as wheat:

32 But I have prayed for thee, that thy faith fail not: and thou, being once converted, confirm thy brethren.

33 Who said to him: Lord, I am ready to go with thee, both into prison, and to death.

34 And he said: I say to thee, Peter, the cock shall not crow this day, till thou thrice deniest that thou knowest me. And he said to them:

35 When I sent you without purse, and scrip, and shoes, did you want anything?

36 But they said: Nothing. Then said he unto them: But now he that hath a purse, let him take it, and likewise a scrip; and he that hath not, let him sell his coat, and buy a sword.

37 For I say to you, that this that is written must yet be fulfilled in me: And with the wicked was he reckoned. For the things concerning me have an end.

38 But they said: Lord, behold here are two swords. And he said to them, It is enough.

vv. 28–30

Our Lord does not say, as He might have done, that the apostles had *continued with* Him in His journeys or works, but *in* His *temptations*, or trials. It was a sign of greater love on their part to have done this. As the moment of parting approaches, He wishes to express His own love more vividly than before, which He does by commending their own.

vv. 31–34

In addressing St Peter as *Simon*, using, so to speak, his personal rather than his papal name, Jesus indicates directly that His prayer was made for St Peter personally. It is St Peter's own *faith* that will *fail not* during the passion, even when his confession of it fails, but nothing is said of the personal faith of his successors. Yet an allusion is made to these successors, in that St Peter is given the office to *confirm* his *brethren*, an office that will necessarily have to be exercised in later ages too. Hence, Christ indirectly indicates that Peter's successors will receive an unerring power to define matters of faith. In predicting the denial, the Lord calls him *Peter*, as if to show that he will not lose this office on account of his sin.

vv. 35–38

In chapter nine, Christ sent the twelve to preach without possessions. Here, He bids them take *purse and scrip*, that is, wallet and bag, and even to acquire a *sword*, and He explicitly contrasts this charge with their previous mission. As if to bid us reflect on the symbolic sense of this episode, He adds: *The things about me have an end*, that is, a goal or purpose. What does it all mean?

According to St Thomas Aquinas, by giving the apostles two such different missions, Christ was signifying two states of the Church: a first, when she would lack the means of temporal support, and a second, beginning from the time when earthly rulers began to convert, when she would now be aided by such means. In the second state, the Church is even to acquire a sword, since though the faith may not be spread by violence or

39 And going out, he went, according to his custom, to the mount of Olives. And his disciples also followed him.

40 And when he was come to the place, he said to them: Pray, lest ye enter into temptation.

41 And he was withdrawn away from them a stone's cast; and kneeling down, he prayed,

42 Saying: Father, if thou wilt, remove this chalice from me: but yet not my will, but thine be done.

43 And there appeared to him an angel from heaven, strengthening him. And being in an agony, he prayed the longer.

44 And his sweat became as drops of blood, trickling down upon the ground.

45 And when he rose up from prayer, and was come to his disciples, he found them sleeping for sorrow.

46 And he said to them: Why sleep you? arise, pray, lest you enter into temptation.

any form of coercion, Catholic rulers may use force to preserve the commonwealth, including its Christianity, against external or internal enemies. These enemies will in turn complain that the Church is betraying the gospel by using such means, and thus Christ in His mystical body *will* again *be reckoned with the wicked.*

We may also say that the Lord bids the apostles to take swords so as to allow Himself to be incorrectly reckoned as a revolutionary, in order to lessen in some small degree the guilt of those who have determined in any case to arrest him.

Since the Church is the city of God on earth, it is right for her to possess *two swords,* namely, the spiritual power of the successors of the apostles, and the temporal power of Catholic rulers. No other form of subjection of one man to his neighbour is necessary on earth, and so having been shown both swords, Jesus tells the apostles: *It is enough.*

vv. 39–46

The *temptation* which the apostles have to ward off by prayer is that of doubting that He is the Son of God, when they see Him apparently helpless and defeated.

What is the *chalice* that He asks His Father to remove, if it be His will? Not His death as such, even though this will be the most grievous of human deaths, owing both to the sensibility to pain of His body, formed by the power of the Holy Spirit, and also to the vision of the sins of men that pierces His soul. His death is the redemption of the world, and the baptism with which He desired to be baptised. But He foresees that because their rulers will reject this redemption, the kingdom of God will be taken from the Jews, and that thus He will be *set for the fall of many in Israel.* In like manner, the prophet Jonas was unwilling to preach repentance to the pagans, dimly foreboding that their repentance would mean the setting aside of his own people; thus, in this way also, Christ becomes *the sign of Jonas* for the men of His time.

He also foresees all the reprobate until the end of the world, who will be made worse and not better by occasion of His death,

47 As he was yet speaking, behold a multitude; and he that was called Judas, one of the twelve, went before them, and drew near to Jesus, for to kiss him.

48 And Jesus said to him: Judas, dost thou betray the Son of man with a kiss?

49 And they that were about him, seeing what would follow, said to him: Lord, shall we strike with the sword?

50 And one of them struck the servant of the high priest and cut off his right ear.

51 But Jesus answering, said: Suffer ye thus far. And when he had touched his ear, he healed him.

52 And Jesus said to the chief priests, and magistrates of the temple, and the ancients, that were come unto him: Are ye come out, as it were against a thief, with swords and clubs?

53 When I was daily with you in the temple, you did not stretch forth your hands against me: but this is your hour, and the power of darkness.

54 And apprehending him, they led him to the high priest's house. But Peter followed afar off.

55 And when they had kindled a fire in the midst of the hall, and were sitting about it,

Peter was in the midst of them.

56 Whom when a certain servant maid had seen sitting at the light, and had earnestly beheld him, she said: This man also was with him.

when they reject the graces that it won for them. Hence the *agony* or contest between His desire to do the Father's will and His desire that not one soul take occasion from His life and death to damn itself.

The *angel from heaven* strengthens Him, since He has willed that His vision of His Father, and the beatific joy that results from it, have no influence, during His passion, on the other thoughts and affections of His soul; and so though even as man He is superior to the angels, He is now able to be strengthened by them. The angel of the agony is perhaps St Gabriel, whose name means 'the strength of God'.

vv. 47–53

Why does St Luke say *he that was called Judas* came with the multitude, rather than simply 'Judas'? Perhaps because though he still bears the name, the man himself has, as it were, disappeared, having surrendered himself up to the power of the enemy.

Christ does not give permission to the apostles to *strike with the sword*, principally because He does not wish to impede the redemption, but also because it was unfitting that they, as priests of the new covenant, should shed blood, and because, as far as the laws of the land were concerned, they were only private individuals. He points out the irrationality of those who have come against Him *with swords and clubs*, and at night, when they could have found Him without any special preparation during the day. He also offers a partial extenuation of their sin: they are under the influence of *the power of darkness*, the devil, to whom His Father has allowed an *hour*, a brief opportunity, to act.

vv. 54–71

St Luke passes briefly over the assemblies, perhaps irregular, that took place that night in the houses of Annas and Caiaphas, and describes in more detail the meeting of the *council* or Sanhedrin, held *as soon as it was day*. No obvious outrage is committed against Him at this meeting: the high priest, now acting in the day-time, had to preserve the appearance of legality.

57 But he denied him, saying: Woman, I know him not.

58 And after a little while, another seeing him, said: Thou also art one of them. But Peter said: O man, I am not.

59 And after the space, as it were of one hour, another certain man affirmed, saying: Of a truth, this man was also with him; for he is also a Galilean.

60 And Peter said: Man, I know not what thou sayest. And immediately, as he was yet speaking, the cock crew.

61 And the Lord turning looked on Peter. And Peter remembered the word of the Lord, as he had said: Before the cock crow, thou shalt deny me thrice.

62 And Peter going out, wept bitterly.

63 And the men that held him, mocked him, and struck him.

64 And they blindfolded him and smote his face. And they asked him, saying:

Prophesy, who is it that struck thee?

65 And blaspheming, many other things they said against him.

66 And as soon as it was day, the ancients of the people, and the chief priests and scribes, cane together; and they brought him into their council, saying: If thou be the Christ, tell us.

67 And he saith to them: If I shall tell you, you will not believe me.

68 And if I shall also ask you, you will not answer me, nor let me go.

69 But hereafter the Son of man shall be sitting on the right hand of the power of God.

70 Then said they all: Art thou then the Son of God? Who said: You say that I am.

71 71 And they said: What need we any further testimony? for we ourselves have heard it from his own mouth.

Why does our Lord not explicitly confess His messiahship before this forum? It is true that He knows that *if* He tells them, they *will not believe*, yet it might still seem the proper place for this all-important declaration to be made. Presumably it would be the right place, had not, as we learn from St Mark, *the chief priests and all the council* already passed the sentence of death upon Him at Caiaphas's bidding during the meeting at night. The council held publicly on the Friday morning was thus a sham: the Defendant and the judge both knew this, and both knew that the other knew it. In such circumstances, Christ might have seemed to countenance a lie by treating the trial as if it were a serious attempt to come to a correct verdict. For this reason, He will not *ask* them the questions that ought to cause them to *let* Him *go*, about the prophecies of the Scriptures and about the testimonies of St John the Baptist and of His miracles.

However, lest He seem to those ignorant of the circumstances to fail to bear witness before the highest court of His people, Jesus testifies to a truth that includes while surpassing that of His messiahship, namely, His divinity. To be *the Son of God* without qualification implies equality to the Father. The words, *You say that I am* are a humble and yet majestic acceptance of this title.

1 And the whole multitude of them rising up, led him to Pilate.

2 And they began to accuse him, saying: We have found this man perverting our nation, and forbidding to give tribute to Caesar, and saying that he is Christ the king.

3 And Pilate asked him, saying: Art thou the king of the Jews? But he answering, said: Thou sayest it.

4 And Pilate said to the chief priests and to the multitudes: I find no cause in this man.

5 But they were more earnest, saying: He stirreth up the people, teaching throughout all Judea, beginning from Galilee to this place.

6 But Pilate hearing Galilee, asked if the man were of Galilee?

7 And when he understood that he was of Herod's jurisdiction, he sent him away to Herod, who was also himself at Jerusalem, in those days.

8 And Herod, seeing Jesus, was very glad; for he was desirous of a long time to see him, because he had heard many things of him; and he hoped to see some sign wrought by him.

9 And he questioned him in many words. But he answered him nothing.

10 And the chief priests and the scribes stood by, earnestly accusing him.

11 And Herod with his army set him at nought, and mocked him, putting on him a white garment, and sent him back to Pilate.

12 And Herod and Pilate were made friends, that same day; for before they were enemies one to another.

13 And Pilate, calling together the chief priests, and the magistrates, and the people,

14 Said to them: You have presented unto me this man, as one that perverteth the people; and behold I, having examined him before you, find no cause in this man, in those things wherein you accuse him.

15 No, nor Herod neither. For I sent you to him, and behold, nothing worthy of death is done to him.

vv. 1–17

OUR LORD ANSWERS PILATE, ALBEIT briefly, to set an example of obedience to *the higher powers*. Since Pilate was Herod's superior, there was no need for Him also to reply to Herod. Herod, also, is not making even a semblance of an attempt to conduct a regular judicial enquiry. He simply wants *to seek some sign*. For this reason also he had no right to be answered. In justice and mercy a sign is denied him. The behaviour of Herod in *mocking* Christ rather than pronouncing a legal verdict shows that he held no trial.

Pilate acts unjustly in determining *to chastise*, that is, scourge, the Lord without having found Him guilty of any crime.

16 I will chastise him therefore, and release him.

17 Now of necessity he was to release unto them one upon the feast day.

18 But the whole multitude together cried out, saying: Away with this man, and release unto us Barabbas:

19 Who, for a certain sedition made in the city, and for a murder, was cast into prison.

20 And Pilate again spoke to them, desiring to release Jesus.

21 But they cried again, saying: Crucify him, crucify him.

22 And he said to them the third time: Why, what evil hath this man done? I find no cause of death in him. I will chastise him therefore, and let him go.

23 But they were instant with loud voices, requiring that he might be crucified; and their voices prevailed.

24 And Pilate gave sentence that it should be as they required.

25 And he released unto them him who for murder and sedition, had been cast into prison, whom they had desired; but Jesus he delivered up to their will.

26 And as they led him away, they laid hold of one Simon of Cyrene, coming from the country; and they laid the cross on him to carry after Jesus.

27 And there followed him a great multitude of people, and of women, who bewailed and lamented him.

28 But Jesus turning to them, said: Daughters of Jerusalem, weep not over me; but weep for yourselves, and for your children.

29 For behold, the days shall come, wherein they will say: Blessed are the barren, and the wombs that have not borne, and the paps that have not given suck.

30 Then shall they begin to say to the mountains: Fall upon us; and to the hills: Cover us.

31 For if in the green wood they do these things, what shall be done in the dry?

vv. 18–31

Although *the whole multitude* demands His crucifixion, this does not mean the whole people absolutely, but rather all those who had gathered for the trial, since *there* also *followed him a great multitude who lamented him.* Why did this second multitude not intervene at the trial? From fear: St John notes that the Jewish authorities had decided that *if any man should confess him to be the Christ, he should be put out of the synagogue,* that is, stripped of his rights as a Jew.

Why does our Lord speak especially to the *women,* when there were also men following Him to Calvary? Perhaps because they were braver in showing their allegiance; perhaps also because He wished to lament over Jerusalem, and a city in the Scriptures being spoken of as feminine is represented more naturally by women than by men. Yet is it not better to *weep over* the passion of Christ than over one's own misfortunes or even those of one's *children,* as being in itself a greater evil? Christ did not wish by these words to stop their tears altogether but to prevent them from lamenting in a despairing way, and also to contrast His readiness to die with the unreadiness with which many of the inhabitants of Jerusalem would meet their death during the great siege.

He quotes the words of the prophet Osee about the *mountains and the hills,* which Osee foretold would be spoken by a people who had not feared the Lord and who had therefore been deprived of their king.

If the Romans have treated with such violence Him who is like *green wood,* having the life-giving Spirit by nature as a tree has its sap, what will they do *in the dry,* that is, to those who are bereft of all grace? For the latter group will not be able to count on divine protection, and they will provoke the imperial wrath directly, rebelling against Rome for earthly reasons.

32 And there were also two other malefactors led with him to be put to death.

33 And when they were come to the place which is called Calvary, they crucified him there; and the robbers, one on the right hand, and the other on the left.

34 And Jesus said: Father, forgive them, for they know not what they do. But they, dividing his garments, cast lots.

35 And the people stood beholding, and the rulers with them derided him, saying: He saved others; let him save himself, if he be Christ, the elect of God.

36 And the soldiers also mocked him, coming to him, and offering him vinegar,

37 And saying: If thou be the king of the Jews, save thyself.

38 And there was also a superscription written over him in letters of Greek, and Latin, and Hebrew: THIS IS THE KING OF THE JEWS.

39 And one of those robbers who were hanged, blasphemed him, saying: If thou be Christ, save thyself and us.

40 But the other answering, rebuked him, saying: Neither dost thou fear God, seeing thou art condemned under the same condemnation?

41 And we indeed justly, for we receive the due reward of our deeds; but this man hath done no evil.

42 And he said to Jesus: Lord, remember me when thou shalt come into thy kingdom.

43 And Jesus said to him: Amen I say to thee, this day thou shalt be with me in paradise.

vv. 32–38

They crucify our Lord in the midst of *two other malefactors*, so that He will be the more looked upon: we naturally look more to the middle of a group.

Whom does our Lord ask His heavenly Father to *forgive*? It does not seem to be the Jewish authorities: for them it is an aggravating and not a mitigating circumstance that they *know not what they do.* Their ignorance was culpable, for it was of them that Christ said to the apostles: *If I had not done among them the works that no other man hath done, they would not have sin.* It seems therefore to be the Roman soldiers for whom He is praying. But if they did not know that He was innocent, and the Son of God, why did they need God to forgive them for carrying out a legal punishment that their commanding officer had assigned to them after a trial by the proper authority? Probably they carried it out with deliberate cruelty, influenced by demons; also, we may suppose that in fact they were culpable for not knowing that He was an innocent man, given His reputation for miracles and the wonderful patience they could themselves see, even if they had not had the same opportunities as the Jewish authorities to learn of His divinity.

The blindness of the *rulers* is shown by their confession that *he saved others.*

vv. 39–43

Christ's prayer for those who *blasphemed him* is answered, even before His death, by the conversion of the good thief. In chapter seven, a centurion had by his faith caused Christ to marvel, but at that time the Lord was followed by an admiring crowd and was still working miracles. The faith of the thief is greater yet, and his reward immediate. He will be with Jesus that day *in paradise,* since his soul will be with the soul of the Logos in the Limbo of the Just, which will become a paradise, since the vision of the Blessed Trinity will be immediately bestowed upon all who are waiting there.

COMMENTARY ON ST. LUKE'S GOSPEL

44 And it was almost the sixth hour; and there was darkness over all the earth until the ninth hour.

45 And the sun was darkened, and the veil of the temple was rent in the midst.

46 And Jesus crying out with a loud voice, said: Father, into thy hands I commend my spirit. And saying this, he gave up the ghost.

47 Now the centurion, seeing what was done, glorified God, saying: Indeed this was a just man.

48 And all the multitude of them that were come together to that sight, and saw the things that were done, returned striking their breasts.

49 And all his acquaintance, and the women that had followed him from Galilee, stood afar off, beholding these things.

50 And behold there was a man named Joseph, who was a counsellor, a good and just man,

51 (The same had not consented to their counsel and doings;) of Arimathea, a city of Judea; who also himself looked for the kingdom of God.

52 This man went to Pilate and begged the body of Jesus.

53 And taking him down, he wrapped him in fine linen, and laid him in a sepulchre that was hewed in stone, wherein never yet any man had been laid.

54 And it was the day of the Parasceve, and the sabbath drew on.

55 And the women that were come with him from Galilee, following after, saw the sepulchre, and how his body was laid.

56 And returning, they prepared spices and ointments; and on the sabbath day they rested, according to the commandment.

vv. 44–49

To teach us that His whole life has been foretold by the psalms, our Lord's last word is a quotation; but He changes the first word from 'Lord' to *Father*, to show that by His death He has made available for all the faithful a filial relationship with His Father that under the old covenant was beyond their reach.

He gave up the ghost. According to St Francis de Sales, Jesus here voluntarily allows the charity of His sacred Heart to produce its natural effect, namely, by the intensity of its impetus to separate His body from His soul. Yet both body and soul remain hypostatically united to the Word.

The centurion knows that dying men cannot naturally cry out *with a loud voice*, and so the manner of Christ's death shows this soldier that God was bearing witness to Christ's innocence.

vv. 50–56

The acquaintances and the women, with the rest of the *multitude, stood afar off,* but as we learn from St John, our Lady and a few others *stood by the cross.*

St *Joseph of Arimathea*, like the spouse of the Blessed Virgin Mary, was *just*. The English poet, Richard Crashaw, a seventeenth-century convert to the Church, fittingly apostrophised Jesus in these words:

> How life and death in thee
>   Agree!
> Thou hadst a virgin womb
>   And tomb.
> A Joseph didst betroth
>   Them both.

It was the day of the Parasceve, that is, of preparation for the Sabbath. Since "the old Law died on the Cross", the *women* were no longer bound by *the commandment* obliging them to rest on the Saturday, but doubtless they were not yet aware of this fact.

1 And on the first day of the week, very early in the morning, they came to the sepulchre, bringing the spices which they had prepared.

2 And they found the stone rolled back from the sepulchre.

3 And going in, they found not the body of the Lord Jesus.

4 And it came to pass, as they were astonished in their mind at this, behold, two men stood by them, in shining apparel.

5 And as they were afraid, and bowed down their countenance towards the ground, they said unto them: Why seek you the living with the dead?

6 He is not here but is risen. Remember how he spoke unto you, when he was in Galilee,

7 Saying: The Son of man must be delivered into the hands of sinful men, and be crucified, and the third day rise again.

8 And they remembered his words.

9 And going back from the sepulchre, they told all these things to the eleven, and to all the rest.

10 And it was Mary Magdalen, and Joanna, and Mary of James, and the other women that were with them, who told these things to the apostles.

11 And these words seemed to them as idle tales; and they did not believe them.

12 But Peter rising up, ran to the sepulchre, and stooping down, he saw the linen cloths laid by themselves; and went away wondering in himself at that which was come to pass.

13 And behold, two of them went, the same day, to a town which was sixty furlongs from Jerusalem, named Emmaus.

14 And they talked together of all these things which had happened.

15 And it came to pass, that while they talked and reasoned with themselves, Jesus himself also drawing near, went with them.

16 But their eyes were held, that they should not know him.

VV. 1–12

E LEARN FROM THE ANGEL'S WORDS THAT Christ had not prophesied His death and resurrection to the apostles alone, but also to the women. The angel reminds them of the fact that this prophecy had been made *when* Jesus *was yet in Galilee*, to reassure them that the Lord had gone to His death freely, and that the events of Good Friday had therefore not been a disaster.

VV. 13–33

Why does St Luke give the name of only one of the *two* disciples travelling to Emmaus? Perhaps because the other was himself, and from modesty he wishes to conceal the fact that he received an apparition from Christ.

It was when they not only *talked* but also *reasoned with themselves* about what they had seen that *Jesus* drew *near*; a sign that

17 And he said to them: What are these discourses that you hold one with another as you walk, and are sad?

18 And the one of them, whose name was Cleophas, answering, said to him: Art thou only a stranger to Jerusalem, and hast not known the things that have been done there in these days?

19 To whom he said: What things? And they said: Concerning Jesus of Nazareth, who was a prophet, mighty in work and word before God and all the people;

20 And how our chief priests and princes delivered him to be condemned to death, and crucified him.

21 But we hoped that it was he that should have redeemed Israel: and now besides all this, today is the third day since these things were done.

22 Yea and certain women also of our company affrighted us, who before it was light, were at the sepulchre,

23 And not finding his body, came, saying, that they had also seen a vision of angels, who say that he is alive.

24 And some of our people went to the sepulchre, and found it so as the women had said, but him they found not.

25 Then he said to them: O foolish, and slow of heart to believe in all things which the prophets have spoken.

26 Ought not Christ to have suffered these things, and so to enter into his glory?

27 And beginning at Moses and all the prophets, he expounded to them in all the scriptures, the things that were concerning him.

28 And they drew nigh to the town, whither they were going: and he made as though he would go farther.

29 But they constrained him; saying: Stay with us, because it is towards evening, and the day is now far spent. And he went in with them.

30 And it came to pass, whilst he was at table with them, he took bread, and blessed, and brake, and gave to them.

31 And their eyes were opened, and they knew him: and he vanished out of their sight.

32 And they said one to the other: Was not our heart burning within us, whilst he spoke in this way, and opened to us the scriptures?

33 And rising up, the same hour, they went back to Jerusalem: and they found the eleven gathered together, and those that were staying with them,

God blesses the efforts of those who apply their minds to understand what pertains to His Son.

From St Mark, we learn that at least part of what prevented the two disciples from recognising Christ at first was that *he appeared in another shape* or form, that is, with His appearance somewhat different to what it had been before the crucifixion. The words of St Luke suggest that there was also some obstacle in the minds of the disciples themselves. St Gregory the Great explains that because they both loved and yet doubted, the Lord both came near them and yet did not show them who He was: thus, what happened without corresponded to what was happening within.[1]

Cleophas speaks truer than he knows. Risen again, Jesus is now *only a stranger in* the earthly *Jerusalem*, foreign to mortality and no longer practising the rites of the old Law.

Having expounded *all the prophets* to them, the Lord *made as if he would go further*, so as to give them the opportunity to prove their gratitude by hospitality.

He does not offer the Eucharistic sacrifice, since no wine is mentioned. Instead, after having explained the Scriptures, He gives them *blessed bread*, perhaps to foreshadow a custom of many churches whereby such bread would be given to those who are not yet ready to receive the Eucharist.

It is not possible to say whether *he vanished out of their sight* by going elsewhere or because their eyes were held from seeing Him still present. But why did He vanish when they had come to believe in the resurrection, given that He had accompanied them when their faith was still imperfect? Perhaps so that their previous fault might be brought home to them more keenly; and also because they would have been less willing to go back to Jerusalem, had He remained. The journey was *sixty furlongs*, that is, seven and a half miles.

---

1 *Homilies on the gospels*, 23.1

34 Saying: The Lord is risen indeed, and hath appeared to Simon.

35 And they told what things were done in the way; and how they knew him in the breaking of the bread.

36 Now whilst they were speaking these things, Jesus stood in the midst of them, and saith to them: Peace be to you; it is I, fear not.

37 But they being troubled and frightened, supposed that they saw a spirit.

38 And he said to them: Why are you troubled, and why do thoughts arise in your hearts?

39 See my hands and feet, that it is I myself; handle, and see: for a spirit hath not flesh and bones, as you see me to have.

40 And when he had said this, he shewed them his hands and feet.

41 But while they yet believed not, and wondered for joy, he said: Have you anything to eat?

42 And they offered him a piece of a broiled fish, and a honeycomb.

43 And when he had eaten before them, taking the remains, he gave to them.

44 And he said to them: These are the words which I spoke to you, while I was yet with you, that all things must needs be fulfilled, which are written in the law of Moses, and in the prophets, and in the psalms, concerning me.

45 Then he opened their understanding, that they might understand the scriptures.

46 And he said to them: Thus it is written, and thus it behoved Christ to suffer, and to rise again from the dead, the third day:

47 And that penance and remission of sins should be preached in his name, unto all nations, beginning at Jerusalem.

48 And you are witnesses of these things.

49 And I send the promise of my Father upon you: but stay you in the city till you be endued with power from on high.

vv. 34–48

The *eleven were gathered together*, but Thomas must have gone out while they were speaking, before Christ came.

When the Lord comes among them, He asks for something *to eat*, not as if food is necessary to a risen body, but to show that His body is still a human one. He did not eat all the *fish* and the *honeycomb*, setting an example of temperance, leaving them *the remains*, so that seeing these later, the disciples might reassure themselves that they had not imagined His coming.

Before the resurrection, He does not appear to have taught them so clearly that the *remission of sins* was to be made available *unto all nations*. This might have appeared too great a miracle, until they had seen Him return from the dead.

vv. 49

The Holy Ghost is called *the promise of* the *Father*, because the Father had promised through the prophets to send His Spirit, and because by possessing Him one is made able to attain all the promises of God, and because He comes forth from the Father through the Word, as our promises come forth through

50 And he led them out as far as Bethania: and lifting up his hands, he blessed them.

51 And it came to pass, whilst he blessed them, he departed from them, and was carried up to heaven.

52 And they adoring went back into Jerusalem with great joy.

53 And they were always in the temple, praising and blessing God. Amen.

our speech. But since the Holy Spirit proceeds also from the Son, why is He not also called "the promise of the Son"? Christ here is actively promising Him, so it was not necessary also to give Him such a name.

The evangelist compresses his account of the forty days between the resurrection and the ascension into a brief space. He could have finished his gospel with the first dozen verses of the Acts of the Apostles, which relate the ascension in greater detail. He seems instead to have wished that the resurrection be the climax of the gospel.

vv. 50–53

St Luke, who especially "directed his intention to the role of the priest", tells us that Christ's final act is the priestly one of *blessing*. But why do the apostles return to *the temple*, since the new covenant is now inaugurated? Although the veil of the covenant has been torn in two, the glory has not yet departed. The temple has achieved that for which it was founded, and as it were in gratitude toward it, the apostles continue to resort there while it stands. This also refutes the error of those today who say that Christ by His death did away with the distinction between the sacred and the profane, and with the need for sacred places.

Having begun in the temple with St Zachary, the evangelist now finishes in the same place, thus making his gospel an image of eternity, where the blessed are *always praising and blessing God. Amen.*

Lightning Source UK Ltd.
Milton Keynes UK
UKHW012348271221
396261UK00011B/356/J